The Viennese Kitchen

The Viennese Kitchen

TANTE HERTHA'S BOOK OF FAMILY RECIPES

Monica Meehan and Maria von Baich

Interlink Books

An imprint of Interlink Publishing Group, Inc.
Northampton, Massachusetts

For Hertha and Lene
To the timeless bond of cousins

First paperback edition published in 2017 by

INTERLINK BOOKS
An imprint of Interlink Publishing Group, Inc.
46 Crosby Street, Northampton, MA 01060
www.interlinkbooks.com

ISBN 978-1-56656-865-4 hardback
ISBN 978-1-56656-019-1 paperback

Publisher: Clare Sayer
Production: Laurence Poos
Design: Jacqui Caulton
Cover Design: Julian D. Ramirez
Americanization: Sara Rauch and Leyla Moushabeck
Food Photography: Tara Fisher
Food Stylist: Annie Rigg
Prop Stylist: Roisin Nield
Location Photography: Jon Meade
Additional Location Photography: Georg von Baich
All historical photographs were accessed from the authors' family's private collection.

1 3 5 7 9 10 8 6 4 2

Printed and bound in Singapore

Contents

Introduction

A Viennese Life

How did *The Viennese Kitchen* come to be? Why Viennese dishes and who was Tante Hertha?

Tante Hertha's story will come. In some subtle respects, the paths that both my mother Maria and I have taken parallel Hertha's, in the uncanny ways a family's history can find common ground decades later. For many years, a faded brown notebook filled with Hertha's beautifully penned collection of Viennese specialties, entries as early as the turn of the twentieth century, written in peaceful as well as troubled times, lay dormant in a kitchen drawer, quietly waiting to be opened again. These recipes have taken their own physical journey across oceans and back again to make their way into this cookbook as an ode to Hertha's Vienna.

To begin, Tante Hertha had not been one of the mythical figures of my childhood. She was to me part of the interesting collection of names about which my beloved Austrian grandmother and her contemporaries that made up a large circle of extended family and friends, spoke warmly: Tante Vera, Onkel Kurt, Otto Mayr, Tante Olga, Duschan, Onkel Anton, Onkel Bruno, Tante Elsa. They were all *Tanten* and *Onkel*, aunts and uncles, for whom I felt no distinct connection apart from what I imagined the holders of these glamorous names and colorful lives represented in the Vienna of their past, from the early 20th century until the end of the 1960s when Vienna was to change for good.

The day our cookbook was contracted, I called my mother's brother Paul and his wife Marie in British Columbia, Canada to tell them about our project. In her charming, soft French-Canadian lilt, my aunt Marie said "this is probably nothing for the book, but I remember the day your grandmother was with us in Montreal in the spring of 1971. She came running into the room filled with tears, clutching a letter from home: '*Tante Hertha*

ist gestorben, Tante Hertha ist gestorben!'"
pronouncing with such heartfelt sorrow that
Tante Hertha had died. Warm but equally
Victorian, my grandmother was not one to
express emotion in such a way. The loss she
felt, in the sad words the letter would have
conveyed, was the beginning of a door slowly
closing on the Vienna of the past. Almost
forty years later, I began to discover who
Hertha may have really been, beyond just
another beautiful and faded name.

Baroness Hertha Freiin von Winkler was
born in Krain (Slovenia today) on the 2nd
of July 1889 at her family home, the Villa
Samassa, but lived for most of her life in
Vienna. Her father was Baron Egon von
Winkler, a high-ranking official in the
Austrian Ministry of the Interior, and her
mother Bertha (née Samassa) part of a wealthy and illustrious family who
manufactured church bells and candelabra, with orders as far-reaching as South
America. Hertha was my grandmother Helene Galle's first cousin; their mothers were
sisters. Although Hertha was over a decade older than my grandmother, the two
youthful and lively cousins were very close. As young women, they would meet
faithfully every winter in Vienna to attend the annual ball season. The house balls, by
exclusive invitation, were a vital part of every young society woman's calendar.

In the summers throughout the 1920s and early 1930s, Hertha would in turn leave
Vienna for long stays at my grandmother's country estate in modern day Slovenia. At
the end of the First World War, Vienna had witnessed the collapse of the monarchy and
crippling unemployment. Food supply was dismal and there had been severe
Hungersnot (food shortages) in post-war Austria, particularly in the cities. Whenever
she could get away from Vienna, Hertha took the opportunity to escape to the
countryside, where prosperity was, for the time being, unwavering.

My grandmother's estate was based in the small hamlet of Freudenthal, meaning
Joyful Valley, bordering the southwestern region of the Ljubljana Marshes, Slovenia.
Originally a monastery, Schloss Freudenthal was a 6,460 square foot building and
spanned 1500 acres of land with vast forests and game for hunting. It was originally the
home of Carthusian monks, built by the Carinthian Duke Bernhard of Spannheim in

Left: Tante Hertha, circa early 1920s.
Right: My grandmother, Helene (center), with her siblings (from left) Onkel Bruno, Tante Christl, Onkel Gert.
Below: My grandfather's brother, Onkel Duschan (driving), his sister Tante Vera, my grandfather Georges behind with his sister, Tante Olga.
Overleaf: Left-hand page: Hertha's birthplace today, the Villa Samassa; Right-hand page: Schloss Freudenthal, my grandmother's family estate. Clockwise: The interior of Freudenthal; my mother, Maria von Baich as a little girl at the house; my grandmother; the view from the approach to the house; the salon.

1255. In the 17th century, it housed a monks' school and a library, which kept numerous valuable manuscripts. In the family since 1836, it was bequeathed to my great grandfather Franz Galle in 1862. The family home in which my grandmother and her four siblings grew up, together with its large staff who ran the grounds, the forestry business, the game farm, and the household, replaced the somberness of the one-time convent with a much more secular vitality. A small chapel however remained intact if infrequently visited.

Far from idle and yet privileged by a charmed life, the two cousins would go horseback riding, play the piano, needlepoint in the garden, read and enjoy the lively banter of generations of family and friends. Space was plentiful and many guests would find their way to the "joyful valley" each summer to visit the Galle family.

My uncle Paul recalled with affection:

"My memories of Tante Hertha go back to the summers we spent in Freudenthal in the mid- to late 1930s right up to the beginning of Second World War. As a niece of Grandmother Elsa Galle, Hertha had strong ties to Freudenthal – so she frequently left Vienna to stay often for weeks at a time. Offering hospitality at a time of moderately paid servants was not much of a problem. I remember her as a very cheerful presence, who loved fun and jokes (which we kids of course didn't get), and enjoying long walks in the fields or forest. Hertha loved visitors, guests and most certainly good food, even if it was prepared by peasant kitchen maids and not up to Viennese society standards."

During the First World War, Hertha was a nurse in a military hospital for the Red Cross. It was hardly a career path but an honorable contribution nonetheless to help in the war effort along with so many other young women. After the war, Hertha, who would have been supported by her mother's modest post-war pension, was eager to consider a job opportunity. There were very few suitable prospects for young ladies, and for someone of

Above: My grandmother, Helene, taken by Hertha. On the bottom right of the image you can just make out Hertha's distinctive embossed signature.

Above right: My grandfather, Georges.

Right: My grandparents' wedding at Schloss Freudenthal.

her social standing, even less so. By chance, one of the new professional possibilities open to women was portrait photography, quickly becoming quite the rage in the 1920s. The training would have been rather basic, but Hertha soon acquired darkroom staff and eventually opened a small atelier on the Graben, one of Vienna's most exclusive and fashionable streets in the first quarter of the city. Her notable *Hertha*, embossed on the lower right hand corner of the heavy photographic placards alongside the studio's address, was an elegant mark of distinction for the intrepid new photographer.

In 1929, my grandparents married at Schloss Freudenthal. The wedding was a formal yet intimate affair with 27 guests gathering together to celebrate the marriage of Helene Galle and Georges von Baich. Helene's beloved cousin Baroness Hertha of course attended. She had photographed the engagement photo earlier in the year in Vienna and now, the gathering itself. It is a photograph I always remember; my great-grandfather with long white beard and

21. April 1929

Hertha

Above: Hertha's invitation to my grandparents' wedding in April 1929. The front shows the engagement portrait, taken by Hertha. The signatures of all the guests are on the back.
Right: Schloss Freudenthal.

dark suit, beautiful women in 1920s flapper fashion, men in top hats and finally Hertha, sitting at the very edge of the photograph, the image a little too faded to see her entirely. The names again – Vera, Olga, Elsa – captured in the still of Hertha's timeless photograph.

The newly married couple had been presented as a wedding gift a house in Laibach (Ljubljana) to start their family, where my mother was born, before moving on to Marburg and ultimately taking refuge with relatives in neighboring Austria. Franz Galle passed away a few years after the wedding. His eldest son Bruno would inherit the entire seat and continue to run Freudenthal, which had only just narrowly survived the 1930s stock market crash. By 1944, Germanic families, in particular wealthy landowners, were forced to leave the Yugoslav state or face a communist regime and a critical fate. Overtaken by state militia with great force and speed in a single night, Bruno and his family were stripped of their home with only a few small possessions between them.

Freudenthal was gone. Its long idle summers remained the sharpest of memories for its one-time inhabitants. By 1951, the estate became and remains home to the government-run Technical Museum of Slovenia. Their website states: 'The museum is divided into forestry, woodworking, fishing,

hunting, electrical, agricultural, textile, printing and transport departments. Take part in Saturday workshops and Sunday demonstrations of old machinery and techniques and the use of tools that were used by our ancestors.'

Hertha's photographic studio in Vienna eventually moved from the first to the fourth quarter, still central but no longer *the* address. By the beginning of the Second World War with many more *Foto Salons* (studios) competing for business, the novelty was gone and the ability to maintain an income-generating business slowly fading away.

Hertha remained unmarried and as she and her widowed mother were in need of reasonable accommodation in hard times, they were, as luck (and status) would have it, resituated in the heart of the city. Hertha's brother-in-law Baron Dr. Otto Mayr was a partner of a successful law firm with offices on the first floor of a building that featured a relatively small but charming living space on the penthouse floor.

Rotenturmstraße 13. There could not have been a better address in Vienna. Set in the very center of the *Ersten Bezirk*, the first quarter, it was still then a Vienna of wealth and nobility, the elite who had all the right contacts to maintain such central address. Just around the corner sits Vienna's largest cathedral, the 14th-century Stephansdom. Today the area is filled with tourists and ubiquitous chain stores. The neighborhood of the 1920s through to the 1950s would have been one of elegant austerity and a purposeful air with neighboring streets of the Graben, the Kärnterstrasse, and the Kohlmarkt notably the most fashionable pedestrian streets in the city. These were the streets of Imperial Vienna, its inner core landmarked by a vast palace, the Hofburg.

The apartment became affectionately nicknamed *Die Gipfelhütte*, the "summit mountain hut," reachable by the unmistakable creaking and clanking and gentle swaying of an old-fashioned lift with decorative iron and glass doors. In order to secure this wonderfully central apartment within the family, Hertha officially "adopted" my grandmother's sister, again with the help of the her brother-in-law just an elevator ride away. The beautiful and equally intimidating Tante Christl Galle became Christine Baronin von Winkler, and joined Hertha at the *Gipfelhütte*. Christl's mother (my great-grandmother) joined her daughter and niece and the three ladies continued to bring a lively mix of friends and family through its doors.

My mother's Vienna was different from that of her siblings Theodor and Paul and certainly from Hertha's, who was a true *Wienerin* – citizen of Vienna. From their adopted home town of Graz, my mother and her two brothers were all at some point students in Vienna, overlapping for a relatively short period in the mid 1950s. Limited means made frequent trips home to the Styrian capital prohibitive and with the two dashing brothers much more preoccupied with the social scene than with the concerns of their little sister, the student years could be lonely at times. Invitations from Hertha would come on occasion but most young students would prefer to spend time with friends rather than two elderly aunts and a grandmother, no matter how engaging. Regardless, in the quiet Sundays, something would always draw my mother to Hertha's graceful neighborhood. There was always life at Hertha's, and just getting within close proximity to the *Gipfelhütte* brought a sense of peace and comfort.

Life at Hertha's meant a sophisticated mix of friends, food, and of utmost importance, the opera. Hertha had a lifelong subscription to the stately Vienna Opera House and was a massive Wagner fan. In the late 1950s, by then approaching her seventies, she thought nothing of sitting for hours and hours (and consecutive days) through *Der Ring der Nibelungen* in its entirety, *Meistersinger*, *Lohengrin,* and *Parsifal* and saving each and every program, collecting the autographs of her favorite opera singers. She would discuss the performance at length afterwards with occasional critical judgements concerning individual artists. Tante Hertha always had strong opinions, outspoken and determined and with an air of finality in her comments. Her own family was highly musical and the family library of sheet music was impressively comprised of pieces noted for four hands. Her father Egon had friends who had played with Schubert; her Uncle Otto had in the meantime become president of the *Musikverein*, the headquarters for the Society of the Friends of Music and home of the Vienna Philharmonic. He became known as the Music Baron among the city's distinguished musical elite.

A life without music was as unimaginable as her other passion: food and cooking. Sometime after the Second World War when Austria was rebuilding, Hertha decided to transpose her passion into a small catering business for family and friends. With her many contacts and cherished recipes, she was always in demand. The income generated afforded Hertha her many travels, often escorted tours throughout Europe to Spain, Portugal, Greece, and Turkey and as far reaching as Morocco.

Hertha's *Gipfelhütte* kitchen was a mansard-style room, which in reality was a bathroom with a full size tub, covered with a table top when not in use and above, an on-demand gas-flame hot water dispenser. It was usually very hot in her "kitchen" and my mother and her brothers can still envision Tante Hertha hunched over a small kitchen table while preparing jams, marmalades, and any *Mehlspeisen* she'd concoct on order for her clientele. The waft of Seville oranges in winter to prepare her Orange Marmalade and the smell of sugar, chocolate, raisins, and nuts used to make wonderful cakes and biscuits resonated throughout the apartment. Whether entertaining or behind the scenes, Hertha's signature large sparkling diamond earrings and equally sparkling bright blue eyes illuminated whichever room she was in.

Despite her liveliness, her regimen was strict. When guests were invited to lunch – never dinner as is customary today – they were immediately seated to an impeccably laid table and were not permitted to leave their seats until the meal was over. Even the youngest of guests could not help clear the table. Hertha was always in charge, every detail perfect.

Uncle Paul, himself a professional landscape photographer who studied graphic design at the prestigious *Graphische Lehr – und Versuchsanstalt* in Vienna, has a recollection from when he was a young boy of nine or ten. It seems to encapsulate the essence of who Hertha was: a modern, independent woman, single, unafraid, adventurous, glamorous, original.

"In the summer 1943 or 1944 Hertha came for a visit to Marburg/Drau (Maribor/Slovenia today), where we lived at the time. She wore a three-quarter length light-colored silk dress, took me for a walk through town, and was apparently happy to have a male companion escorting her, for, being a hot afternoon, she felt like going into a pub for a beer! Since I had never seen an elegant, white-haired lady with prominent diamond earrings enjoying a beer in a place crammed with teamsters and other working class people, I remember the picture vividly."

My mother is the true cook in this cookbook. As a schoolgirl, she had spent the beginning of her school years at the Sacré-Coeur in Graz, a Catholic private girls' convent school. For the remaining four years of high school, my grandmother felt it would be beneficial to round out her

Hertha's cousin, my grandmother, Helene Galle, circa 1918–1920.

education in a school that while academic enough to provide a diploma towards entering higher education, focused its curriculum on running a household which, of course, meant learning how to cook. Located on a small square on the *Entenplatz* (Duck Place), the "duck school" was a kind of finishing school filled with clichés of city girls quick to snicker at a teacher's provincial accent or pedestrian style as young teenaged girls with a naïve snobbishness were likely to do. The students would gather in groups of three once a week to plan a menu and prepare the dishes of the day, starting with a light entrée and eventually graduating to a more intricate selection by the end of term. My mother deeply resented being enrolled in a school referred to in jest as the *Kochlöffel Akademie* – the Cooking Spoon Academy. She said laughingly that her "cooking spoon" education entitled her to co-author this book.

Growing up, I didn't spend hours in the kitchen at home with my mother licking the icing off a cooking spoon (an Austrian mother would never allow such wastefulness) or learning how to make classic tortes and strudels. In the year spent writing the book, these missing hours in the kitchen were made up over a stove and a laptop learning about the nuances of Viennese cooking by watching, assisting and typing in the savored ingredients and intricate methods dictated by my mother. My favorite recipe had always been *Tante Hertha's Geburtstagstorte*, not realizing the significance the recipe would hold. I had lived with my grandmother for a year as a university student and the lifelong friends I made remember the special birthday cake too. Hertha's recipes had no true how-to instructions as the methodology was assumed, no measurements of a cake pan or speed setting of an electric mixer and certainly no oven temperatures! Once again, my mother's earlier training and natural culinary talent enabled her to interpret and not simply transcribe these dishes.

In 1959, at the age of 22, my independently-minded mother traveled to Canada by ship, with the intention of staying one year to gain foreign work experience in her chosen profession. She returned to Austria at the end of her year abroad with the ultimate realization that it was to say goodbye to her home country and start a new life in Hamilton, Ontario. As always, she curtsied to her grandmother and hand-kissed Hertha, bidding them adieu one final time.

My mother has never lost her Austrian heritage: her precision for detail, her love of music, her experiences from the Cooking Spoon Academy on Duck Place, and her recollections of her short but impactful time in Vienna.

Hertha had added recipes to the old, brown hardcover notebook throughout her adult life. The actual recipe book still exists, featuring several different handwritings, likely a few entries from Hertha's mother, Hertha herself, and possibly those of another aunt or grandmother. A few forgotten receipts and postcards were left gently dotted throughout its pages. When my own grandmother died in 1992, my aunt Ina asked my mother if she would look through a box of old papers and notes that she wasn't intending to keep. In it, was the slightly yellowed recipe book, still intact despite being abandonned for some time. My mother remembered it from many years ago, kept in my grandmother's kitchen drawer and used only for special occasions as an ode to Tante Hertha and her esteemed Viennese style.

A small but invaluable treasure, my mother was delighted to inherit the journal and bring it back home to Toronto that year. Four years ago, when I purchased a small flat in London, my mother brought the book to me as a housewarming gift.

I was too young to have met Tante Hertha. I was however a guest of the Rotenturmstraße on my trips to Vienna. As a young girl, I remember having to courtesy to the revered Tante Christl. I recall the iron clad elevator and the smells of a gas cooker and incredible scent of the freshly made Austrian *Kipferl* from the corner bakery of my grandmother's flat in Graz, and the colorful pink and gold packages of hazelnut waters packed in my grandmother's suitcase when she came to Canada to visit for the summers. And the handwritten letters on light blue airmail paper, tissue paper-thin and covered with a fine ink pen and distinct European handwriting.

As I walk through my own neighborhood in London, past stately Georgian homes and Victorian mansion blocks, I think how surreal it feels to be living in the UK (where my father was born), at the edge of the divide between the past and the present, remembering these Austrian moments so vividly. We have immensely enjoyed our very personal project to retrace Hertha's path and as a result, to rediscover mine and my mother's, each of us with overlapping geographies but very different experiences and timelines. As always, the culture of food unites us and the family and friends with whom we share it, binds us.

Tante Hertha, circa 1940.

Background

A VIENNESE TAPESTRY

If youth knew; if age could.

SIGMUND FREUD

Hertha's Vienna spanned the years between the 1890s through to the end of the 1960s, a most remarkable time in the city's history. The longtime capital of a large multi-national empire under the German-speaking Habsburg dynasty for five centuries, Vienna after 1918 became the capital of the small Republic of Austria. With a population of 1.9 million, the city of Vienna housed 28 percent of the country's entire population by 1934. 1900s Vienna was the age of some of the most formidable artists and intellectuals in modern European history, home to a wealth of celebrated writers, artists, musicians, and scholars.

Modern Vienna was also a place of unmitigated horrors and tragedy. In 1938, the Jewish population in Vienna was estimated at 170,000 and including those of mixed Jewish-Christian background and converts from Judaism, it may have been as high as 200,000, making up more than 10 percent of the city's inhabitants. Thousands witnessing the looming threat of anti-Semitic sentiment emigrated at this time, including an elderly Dr Sigmund Freud, the inventor of psychoanalytic thought, who in June 1938 left the foreboding doom of his cherished Vienna aboard the Orient Express and moved to Hampstead, London for what was to be the last year of his life.

By the summer of 1939, hundreds of Jewish-owned factories and thousands of businesses had been closed or confiscated by the government who had introduced anti-Jewish legislation to extinguish any cultural or economic growth within the community.

All in all, the SS and police deported some 47,555 Austrian Jews to concentration camps in the east. The vast majority of the deportees, along with approximately 18,000 refugees to Austria, were murdered during the Holocaust. Today the Viennese Jewish population is estimated at around 10,000. No more than 1,000 of them were Holocaust survivors.

From the late-18th through to the mid-19th century, Vienna was the musical capital of Europe. Austrian composers Haydn, Mozart, Schubert, Brahms, Strauss, and composer and conductor Gustav Mahler, along with the Vienna Philharmonic and the Vienna Boys Choir, founded in 1498, preceded modern day Vienna. By the arrival of the new century, nothing could eclipse these magnificent forefathers but the new shining stars had become the musicians, conductors, actors, and actresses who interpreted their timeless and magical works. Hertha would have surely many times heard Irmgard Seefried, a German soprano of Austrian parentage who in 1943 made her debut at the Vienna State Opera performing as Eva in Wagner's *Die Meistersinger*, and who remained part of its ensemble until her retirement in 1976. With a completely natural delivery, her warm tone and appealing personality made her a much-celebrated star.

Austrian conductors such as Karl Böhm, Herbert von Karajan, Wilhelm Furtwängler and pianists Friedrich Gulda and Alfred Brendel were, by the mid-twentieth century, taking the classical music world by storm and fêted with great reverence in New York, Berlin, and London. Von Karajan's obituary in *The New York Times* described him as "probably the world's best-known conductor and one of the most powerful figures in classical music."

In art and design, The Vienna Secession, co-founded by Gustav Klimt and Joseph Maria Olbrich, and *Jugendstil* (the German equivalent to *art nouveau*) art movements dominated the age between 1897 and the early 1900s. There were also the city's prominent architectural giants. Otto Wagner designed the Karlsplatz Pavilions, a stylish pair of underground railway exits on the Karlsplatz with sunflower motifs and green copper roofs. His Wagner Pavilions and the Kirche am Steinhof are equally awe-inspiring. Adolf Loos designed in splendid elegance Loos Haus, a fomer tailoring firm, and the American Bar in 1908, a tiny space with floors and ceilings feature layers of dark marble and black onyx, making this a dark little gem of a bar quite ahead of its time.

In the early twentieth century, playwright and novelist Arthur Schnitzler shocked audiences when his play *Der Reigen* was first performed. A series of 10 dialogues, every act focuses on the erotic desires of each of its ten characters. Schnitzler originally only printed 200 copies in 1903 for his fellow writers in the coffeehouses. In 1920 the play was performed for the first time in Hungary as it was banned by the state in Vienna and Leipzig once the nature of the play had been revealed, and therefore could not be

performed at home. It was filmed as *La Ronde* by Max Ophüls in 1950. Stefan Zweig was another highly accomplished writer of the era. Born into the Viennese bourgeoisie in 1881, Zweig won a poetry prize in his ambitious early years and went on to become a prolific and much-translated novelist, essayist, dramatist, and librettist, as well as a renowned translator, and the author of a late autobiography, poignantly named *The World of Yesterday*, written while he was in transcontinental flight from the disaster unfolding in central Europe.

Throughout the era, Austria's class system, determined by social status and not necessarily wealth, remained strong among the multi-tiered aristocrats and upper class families within its society. Viennese women of this milieu had an elegant but always understated air with a uniform of conservative grace, impeccably dressed each day in a handmade skirt and blouse (never trousers!), ironed with a gently starched collar and worn with perfectly polished shoes with a moderate heel. For a more formal luncheon, a light wool suit was often worn, adorned with a tasteful broach. Wearing too much or precious jewelry would be considered vulgar; evening was the time for heirlooms to sparkle. Women in their advanced years would put on their chokers made of small beads woven into a broad band, which would disguise somewhat less youthful necks.
Right up to the 1960s, gloves were always worn when stepping out, even during the warm summer months; beautifully handcrafted in ecru or white, crocheted of fine cotton thread, not reaching beyond one's wrist.

My mother recalls a cocktail dress that my grandmother – by nature an excellent seamstress – had made for her in the 1950s, a charming recollection of a strict mother trying to accept her daughter's modern vision:

"Having searched through rolls upon rolls of material in every retail store, I finally discovered the perfect shade and texture of a warm mocha silk duchesse; it took some persuasion for Mami to give her consent. Then, we had to come to the mutual agreement on design: there was not a single pattern suitable for our ideas so Mami would make her own and after many tearful fittings, the outcome of her enduring labour of love was splendid! A simple bodice with a wide decolleté, short sleeves and a skirt, gathered into tiny pleats just below the waistline, reaching mid-calf. Up to this day, I wish that masterpiece was still around; a sweet memory, in the way in which only women can reminisce about certain exquisite pieces from a past wardrobe."

The little black dress had also made its entry, with the gentle gray flannel dresses being of equal elegance and more often than not worn by the conservative elite. Dressmakers were kept busy either by creating new clothes, or just as frequently making alterations to existing items that would be worn for decades.

The etiquette of a social invitation as seemingly simple as lunch was also steeped in protocol. When invited, most typically for 12:30pm, unwavering punctuality was expected. One would present the hostess with a pretty but, as ever, classic bouquet of flowers or a small bombonière of the finest truffles – as few as two or three was most appropriate as they were sure to be beautifully wrapped from a fine chocolatier. Wine was unheard of as an offering. If flowers were presented, any floral wrapping would be removed before reaching the door. The meal, served on arrival, may have lasted for about an hour, followed by a coffee and small dessert and then leaving your hosts for a *Verdaungschlaf* (digestion nap) shortly after 2pm. Lunches were held during the week as weekends were mostly reserved for family. In the week, offices and stores were closed for business between 12:30pm until 3pm so it was not unusual to see both men and women lunching in this way. With the advent of phones, guests would follow up early the next morning with a gracious call (once phones were commonplace) of appreciation. Phone exchanges remained brief as even local calls were costly. For a larger gathering or special occasion, a handwritten thank-you note was mailed without delay.

After the Second World War, Vienna was split among the Allies until 1955 when Austria regained its independence. By the end of the 1960s, Vienna had become one of the most sophisticated European old-world cities, drawing thousands to the capital every year. For insiders, no one could specify what had changed, but only that it had.

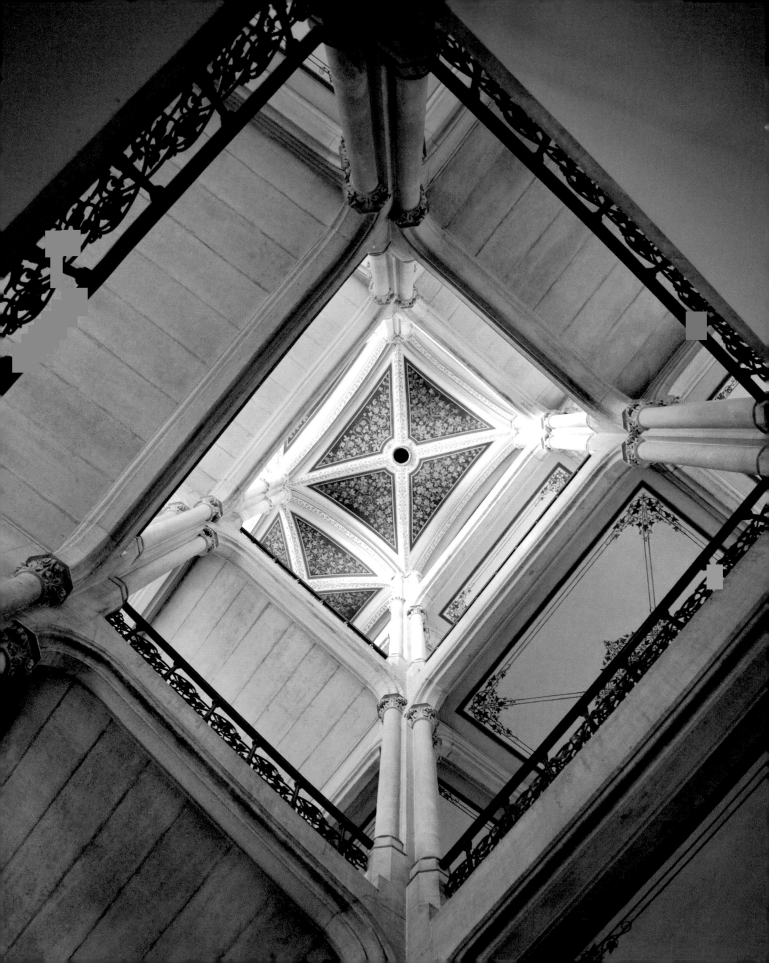

Vorspeisen

APPETIZERS

In April 1929, my grandparents were married in the chapel of my grandmother's family home on the outskirts of Ljubljana, Slovenia. The estate, set in a former cloister, was called *Freudenthal*, which loosely translates as "joyful valley." It was indeed a very joyous time, as twenty-nine friends and family members, resplendent in their silks, pearls and top hats, were presented with an elegant country menu, prepared by the bustling cooks who ran the large household.

Each guest received a place card. The front of the card features an engagement photo of my grandparents which had been taken in Hertha's atelier in Vienna. The wedding menu is outlined on the inside of the card. The selections are a reflection of food that would have been sophisticated dishes of the era — simple by today's standards but noble in their time. The eight-course menu begins with a soup followed by a fish and mayonnaise entrée before continuing with the meat courses, a salad, ice cream, and finally seasonal fruit, exemplifying the fresh ingredients that were easily available and plentiful.

Appetizers were traditionally reserved for formal or festive gatherings. In Hertha's recipe collection, she includes egg dishes such as baked béchamel eggs, fish, cold meats and pâtés, and several dishes referred to, even in the German, as *puddings*, a kind of casserole with meat or noodle-based ingredients.

My grandmother kept Hertha's place card, which we found among her treasured correspondence after many decades. On the back, the signatures of all the guests remain intact.

Fischröllchen

FISH CROQUETTES

MAKES 24/SERVES 6

FOR THE FISH

2¼ lb fish of choice, whole or fillets (cod is good)

Sunflower oil, for greasing

Salt and freshly ground pepper

A few sprigs of parsley

1 clove of garlic, peeled

Wedge of fennel (optional)

3 lemon slices

3 sprigs of fresh dill (optional)

1 large egg

2 anchovy fillets, mashed

3 tbsp vegetable oil

½ small onion, peeled and finely chopped

FOR THE BÉCHAMEL SAUCE

⅔ cup milk

3 tbsp/1½ oz butter

½ cup all-purpose flour

Salt

FOR THE COATING

⅓ cup all-purpose flour, seasoned with salt and freshly ground pepper

2 large eggs, lightly beaten

4 oz breadcrumbs

1¼ cups sunflower oil, for frying

Preheat the oven to 180°F/350°C.

If using a whole fish, skin and bone it, and cut it into chunks. Place the fish pieces in a shallow, lightly oiled, ovensafe dish. Cover with a sprinkling of salt and pepper, a few sprigs of parsley, the garlic clove and fennel bulb wedge, if using, and the lemon slices. Drizzle with a little more oil. Additional herbs, such as dill, may also be used if desired. Cover with a sheet of aluminum foil and bake for 15–20 minutes.

Remove the fish from the oven and flake it into smallish pieces, using a fork.

To make the béchamel sauce, start by warming the milk in a saucepan. In a separate medium-size saucepan, melt the butter over medium heat. Stir in the flour, which will be quickly absorbed by the butter. Gradually add the warm milk to the flour mixture, stirring vigorously and constantly until all the milk has been used and the mixture comes to a boil – this should take about 5 minutes. When the sauce appears smooth, season with salt and cook for another few minutes, stirring all the time. Remove from heat and set aside to cool. When the sauce has cooled, add the egg and mix in the flaked fish and anchovy fillets.

Heat the vegetable oil in a frying pan and gently fry the onion until golden. Add to the fish mixture and season to taste.

Using your hands, form sausage-shaped croquettes of the fish mixture approximately 3 inches long and 1 inch in diameter.

You will need three plates: place the seasoned flour in the first, the lightly beaten eggs in the second and the breadcrumbs in the third. Coat each croquette first in the flour, then in the egg, and lastly in the breadcrumbs.

Preheat the oven to 325°F/160°C. Heat the oil in a large frying pan and fry the croquettes in batches until golden brown. Carefully remove them from the pan with kitchen tongs and place on paper towels to drain. Keep the batches warm in the oven, leaving the oven door slightly ajar until all the croquettes have been made.

Gebackene Wurströllchen

DEEP-FRIED SAUSAGE ROLLS

SERVES 4

FOR THE SAUSAGE MEAT

7 oz sausages (Polish or any cured sausage of your choice)

2 tsp sunflower oil, for frying

½ small onion, peeled and finely chopped

½ cup plus 1 tbsp all-purpose flour

½ cup milk

1½ tbsp/¾ oz butter

Pinch of salt

1 large egg yolk, plus ½ a whole egg, if required

1 tsp baking powder

FOR THE COATING

2 heaped tbsp all-purpose flour

1 large egg, lightly beaten

3½ oz breadcrumbs

⅔ cup sunflower oil, for frying

Remove the casing from the sausages, and cut them into small pieces. Pulse in a food processor until coarsely chopped.

Heat the oil in a frying pan and gently fry the onion until lightly golden. Set aside.

Sift the flour into a bowl.

Pour the milk into a stainless steel saucepan, add the butter and salt, and slowly bring to a boil, removing from the heat just as it comes to a boil. Immediately beat in the flour, using a wooden spoon. Beat until the mixture is smooth and pulls away from the pan, leaving the pan "clean." Return the pan to a very low heat and continue to stir vigorously for another 30 seconds. Remove from the heat and allow to cool slightly.

Add the egg yolk, fried onion, baking powder, and ground sausage meat to the pan. If the mixture is too stiff, add half a whole egg, lightly beaten, so that the mixture is still fairly thick and is of the consistency of pliable dough. Shape the dough into sausages 3 inches long and 1 inch in diameter.

You will need three plates. Place the flour in the first, the lightly beaten egg in the second, and the breadcrumbs in the third. Coat each sausage first in the flour, then in the egg, and lastly in the breadcrumbs.

Heat the oil in a heavy-base frying pan and fry the breaded sausages on medium to high heat until golden on all sides. Carefully remove them from the pan with kitchen tongs and place on paper towels to drain.

Gefüllte Eier à la Christoph

STUFFED EGGS À LA CHRISTOPH

SERVES 6

6 large eggs

2 tsp salt

2–3 tbsp mayonnaise,
to taste

2–3 tsp Dijon mustard,
to taste

6–12 drops Tabasco sauce

Paprika, for dusting

Make sure the eggs are at room temperature. Fill a pan large enough to comfortably hold the eggs with cold water, and carefully place the eggs in the pan. Add the salt to the water (this will help with peeling them later) and bring the water to a rapid boil. At that point, remove the pan from the heat and let the eggs sit in the pan, covered, for 30 minutes exactly. This will hard-boil the eggs without overcooking them and leaving an unattractive grey edge around the yolk.

Rinse the eggs in ice cold water. Once the eggs have cooled to room temperature, peel them.

Slice the eggs in half lengthwise and carefully transfer the yolks into a mixing bowl (try very gently pinching the base of the egg and the yolk will come out quite easily). Mash the yolks with a fork and mix in the mayonnaise, mustard, and Tabasco sauce.

Fill the halved egg whites with the yolk mixture using either a teaspoon or a piping bag fitted with a large nozzle. Sprinkle with paprika. The eggs can be made in advance and refrigerated. Remove from the fridge 30 minutes before serving. Keeps for up to two days.

NOTE

The quantities for the mayonnaise, mustard, and Tabasco sauce depend on taste and your own preference for the consistency of the filling. We don't like it too runny, so we use the lower quantity of mayonnaise. For a bit of extra bite, use the higher quantities of mustard and Tabasco sauce.

Käseauflauf

CHEESE SOUFFLÉ

SERVES 4

1½ tbsp/¾ oz unsalted butter

½ cup all-purpose flour

2 cups whole milk

7 oz Emmental cheese, grated

½ tsp salt

3 large egg yolks

4 large egg whites

½ tsp paprika

Butter for greasing
soufflé dish

Preheat the oven to 400°F/200°C.

Heat the butter in a saucepan on medium heat and stir in the flour using a wooden spoon. Gradually add the milk while stirring steadily. The mixture will at first appear a little lumpy, and at this stage you may wish swap your wooden spoon for a whisk. Whisk constantly until the milk comes to a boil. Boil for a few minutes, stirring all the while, until you get a smooth sauce.

Remove the pan from heat and stir in the grated cheese. Return the pan to medium heat and bring the mixture back to a boil, then remove from the heat. Season with salt and set aside to cool. Once cooled, beat in the egg yolks, one at a time, and add a dash of paprika.

In a bowl, whisk the egg whites until stiff and fold them into the mixture. Grease a 9-inch round ovensafe dish, pour in the mixture, and bake for 15 minutes (check the soufflé without opening the oven door at this point and if it has not risen, leave for another few minutes), then lower the oven temperature to 350°F/180°C, and bake for another 5 minutes. Don't expect the dish to rise as high as a standard French style soufflé — it is a less elevated but equally tasty affair. Serve immediately.

Schinkenkipferln
CRESCENTS WITH HAM FILLING

MAKES 12/SERVES 4

FOR THE DOUGH

¼ lb medium-size floury potatoes

¾ cup/3½ oz all-purpose flour, plus extra for dusting

7 tbsp/3½ oz chilled butter, cut into chunks

1 tsp salt, or less if the ham is very salty

FOR THE FILLING

5 oz smoked ham

2 oz bacon

1 large egg white

Wash and steam the potatoes in a steamer rather than in water; this will prevent the potatoes from absorbing too much water and becoming mushy. Drain and cool.

Once cooled, peel the potatoes and press them through a potato ricer. Flour your work surface, keeping a liberal amount of extra flour to hand.

Pour the flour onto the work surface and add the chunks of butter to it. Add the cold pressed potatoes and the salt and work everything together as quickly as possible to form a smooth dough. Shape the dough into a ball and refrigerate for 30 minutes.

Meanwhile, line a baking tray with parchment paper and preheat the oven to 450°F/230°C. While the oven is heating up, make the filling. Chop the ham and bacon into cubes, place in a food processor and pulse until fairly fine. Set aside.

Take half of the dough (keeping the other half in the fridge) and roll it out onto a well-floured surface to ½-inch thick. This will require frequent turning and dusting with a liberal amount of flour, so that it does not stick to the surface.

Cut into 5-inch squares, place a heaped tablespoon of the ham/bacon mixture into the center of each square. Fold one corner diagonally over the mixture to the other corner and press down to seal. Pinch the remaining two corners together and along the seams and fold them towards each other, to form a crescent shape. Lift each crescent onto the baking sheet. Brush egg white evenly over the crescents and bake for 25–30 minutes, until golden brown. Repeat with remaining dough and proceed as above. These crescents taste best eaten immediately, while still warm.

Suppen und Einlagen

SOUPS AND ACCOMPANIMENTS

The presence of a freshly made soup at a Viennese table cannot be underestimated. Many years ago, my great-uncle Bruno had been invited to a formal gathering where an elaborate meal was served. When he returned home, his wife asked about the meeting, eager to hear who had attended and what had been served. "Everything was very good, but the most important thing was missing." "Oh, and what was this?" enquired my aunt with great curiosity. "The soup," declared Uncle Bruno with even greater conviction.

A soup is just as important a course as the main dish; it needs to be just right. A more formal meal always begins with soup. It is presented at the table in an elegant soup terrine. A matching *service* (dinner set) of fine porcelain soup plates — much shallower than ordinary soup bowls — allow just the right amount to be served. Second helpings are never offered (and certainly never requested!) and despite the presence of beautiful salt and pepper servers, it would be considered disrespectful to your hostess to add another pinch or two.

Dunkle Rindsuppe

BEEF CONSOMMÉ

MAKES 8 CUPS

4½ lb beef bones

1 large onion, peeled and quartered

2 large carrots, peeled and cut into 1-inch chunks

1½ oz parsley root, sliced

1½ oz celeriac, coarsely chopped

½ parsnip, roughly chopped (optional)

2 celery stalks, including the leaves, cut into 2-inch pieces

Green tops of 2 leeks, sliced into 2-inch lengths

3 sprigs parsley

1 large tomato, coarsely chopped

3 bay leaves

1 tbsp salt

½ tsp dried thyme or 1 sprig of fresh thyme

10 peppercorns

1 clove of garlic, peeled

Preheat the oven to 400°F/200°C.

Wipe the bones with a moist paper towel and place them in a roasting pan. Roast for 50–60 minutes, turning regularly, until they begin to brown and start rendering fat.

Add the onion, carrots, parsley root, celeriac, and parsnip to the pan, and brown for about 15 minutes. Watch that they do not become too dark!

Transfer the contents of the roasting pan into a large pot, discarding the fat from the pan, and set aside.

Place the roasting pan on the stovetop over medium heat. Pour in a scant ½ cup of cold water, scraping and stirring vigorously, and bring the liquid to a boil. Remove from the heat and add this liquid to the large pot with the remaining ingredients. Add 13 cups of water and bring to a boil, uncovered. Immediately reduce the heat and simmer gently, covered, for 3–4 hours.

Strain and taste the stock. If the flavor is not strong enough, boil for a little longer, uncovered, until the juice becomes more concentrated.

Grießnockerln

SEMOLINA DUMPLINGS

SERVES 4

3½ tbsp/2 oz butter, at room temperature

2 large eggs

Scant 1 cup coarse semolina

½ tsp salt

Put the butter in a bowl and whisk until creamed, using an electric mixer. Adding one egg at a time, continue whisking so that the mixture becomes light and fluffy. Add the semolina, salt, and 2 tablespoons of water, and mix by hand until the batter is well blended. Set aside for 1 hour.

In a large pan, bring a generous amount of salted water to a boil. Take a teaspoon of the batter and use a second teaspoon to cup the batter and round out the dumpling, to create an even oval shape. Work quickly and drop the dumplings into the boiling water until all the batter has been used up. Reduce the temperature to a simmer and cook for 8–10 minutes, then remove the pan from the heat and let the dumplings stand in the water for another 5 minutes.

These dumplings are traditionally added to a good beef stock, such as the Beef Consommé on page 42, just before serving.

Lebernockerln

LIVER DUMPLINGS IN BEEF CONSOMMÉ

SERVES 4

2 stale bread rolls

5 oz calves liver

2 tbsp/1 oz butter or lard

1 small onion, peeled and finely chopped

1 clove of garlic, peeled and minced

3 tbsp finely chopped flat-leaf parsley

Pinch of dried marjoram

Pinch of freshly ground pepper

½ tsp salt

1 large egg

½ cup/2 oz fine fresh breadcrumbs

4 cups beef stock

Chopped chives, to garnish

Cut the bread rolls into thin slices and pour over approximately ½ cup cold water to soften them. Grind the liver: a food processor with a blade attachment works well; pulse, rather than blend on a constant speed.

Melt the butter (or other fat) and fry the onion with the garlic until transparent. Add the parsley and remove the pan from the heat.

Squeeze the excess water from the rolls. Crumble the softened rolls into the onion mixture and add all remaining ingredients (minus the beef stock and chopped chives), mixing well. If the mixture appears too soft, add a few more breadcrumbs. Set aside for 20 minutes, then form the mixture into 2-inch balls (make sure your hands are wet to avoid the mixture sticking to them).

Bring the beef stock to a boil and gently ease the dumplings into the boiling stock. Reduce the heat to a simmer and cover as soon as the liquid begins to come to another boil. Barely simmer for about 15 minutes.

Spoon the dumplings into soup plates and then pour the beef stock over them. Garnish with chopped chives.

Krensuppe
CREAM OF HORSERADISH SOUP

SERVES 4

1 lb floury potatoes

2 medium onions

3 tbsp/1½ oz butter

Scant 2 cups clear vegetable stock

Scant 1 cup low-sodium chicken stock

1 cup whipping cream

1 large egg yolk

2 tbsp white wine

1½ oz fresh horseradish, very finely grated (use a zester)

Salt and freshly ground pepper

Freshly chopped dill, to garnish

Wash, peel and cut the potatoes into ½-inch cubes and coarsely chop the onions. Heat the butter in a large stockpot over low to medium heat until bubbling. Add the potatoes and the onions, and increase the heat to medium, stirring occasionally until the onions turn just translucent, but not mushy and certainly not browned.

Add the vegetable and chicken stocks to the pot, cover, and bring to a boil. Reduce the heat to low-medium and simmer until the potatoes are tender, which should take about 20 minutes.

Remove the pot from the heat and purée the contents directly in the pot using a hand-held blender. Return the pot to medium heat and stir in the whipping cream, increasing the heat a little to bring to a gentle but not rolling boil. Now remove from the heat. In a bowl, whisk the egg yolk with the wine and stir into the hot soup.

Finally, stir in the horseradish and season to taste, but do test the soup first, since the stock may already contain enough salt. Serve hot and sprinkle the chopped dill over each soup plate.

NOTE

For a decadent and stylish touch, pour the whipping cream into ice cube trays and freeze. Remove when the soup is being served, adding one iced "dollop" per serving.

Linsensuppe
LENTIL SOUP

SERVES 6

2 tbsp vegetable oil

1½ oz smoked bacon, diced

2 medium carrots, cut into ½-inch cubes

1 leek, white part only, rinsed and sliced

1 oz celeriac, cut into ½-inch cubes

1 oz parsley root, cubed

¼ parsnip, peeled and cubed

3½ oz Puy lentils, rinsed

½ tsp salt

1 tbsp fresh flat-leaf parsley, finely chopped

Freshly ground pepper

3 cups chicken stock, preferably homemade

1 tsp (or more, to taste) freshly squeezed lemon juice

OPTIONAL

¼ lb hot dogs, cooked gently (do not boil or they will burst), skinned and cut into 1-inch slices

Pour the oil into a large stockpot and heat over medium to high heat. Add the bacon and cook for about 2 minutes, stirring regularly, until the bacon becomes crisp, but not brown.

Stir in the cubed/sliced root vegetables. Sauté for 2 minutes, until the vegetables begin to soften. Add the lentils, salt, flat-leaf parsley, and a few grindings of pepper. Cover and reduce the heat to medium-low. Sauté for another 5 to 8 minutes, checking to make sure that the mixture isn't sticking to the bottom of the pot.

Uncover, pour in the chicken stock along with 2 cups water, and bring to a boil. Cover again and allow the soup to simmer for about 1¼ hours, until the lentils are cooked.

Remove the pot from the heat and allow to cool slightly before puréeing two-thirds of the soup in a blender for a smoother consistency. Return the puréed soup to the stockpot with the remaining unblended soup. Add lemon juice to taste and if desired, the hot dogs. At this point, the consistency of the soup may need adjusting and a little more water added for a thinner soup. The soup will keep refrigerated in an airtight container for several days. When reheating, do so over medium rather than high heat.

Schwammerlsuppe

CREAM OF MUSHROOM SOUP

SERVES 4

FOR THE MUSHROOMS

1½ tbsp/¾ oz butter

½ medium onion, peeled and very finely chopped

1 clove of garlic, peeled and minced

2 heaped tbsp finely chopped parsley

5 oz fresh mushrooms, very thinly sliced (white button mushrooms are standard but a mix of chanterelles and porcini is best)

FOR THE ROUX

2 tbsp dried wild mushrooms (a combination of chanterelles and porcini is ideal)

4 tbsp butter

4 tbsp all-purpose flour

Salt and freshly ground pepper

4 tbsp sour cream

To prepare the mushrooms, melt the butter over medium heat in a large, heavy-base frying pan until bubbling. Add the onion and garlic, and stir gently until the onion is translucent but not yet beginning to color. Add the parsley and the mushrooms, stirring to coat evenly. Fry over low to medium heat until all the moisture has evaporated. Set aside but do not cover with a lid.

To make the roux, pulse the dried wild mushrooms in a clean coffee grinder. Transfer to a heatproof bowl, pour over 1 cup of boiling water, and soak for 30 minutes.

Melt the butter in a large stockpot over medium to high heat until it begins to bubble. Add the flour all at once and stir until it begins to foam. Now add just under 4 cups of boiling water, one cup at a time, while stirring vigorously to avoid any lumps from forming. Continue in this manner until all the water has been used. Add the dried mushrooms and the juice they have been soaking in. Increase the heat to bring the soup to a rolling boil, then reduce to a simmer, cover the pot with a well-fitting lid, and cook for 30 minutes.

Now add the fried mushrooms to the stockpot and cook on a low simmer for another 15 minutes. If the soup is too thin, remove the lid and simmer for a little longer. Season to taste with salt and pepper (if the salt is added too soon, the mushrooms can become rubbery).

In a small bowl, take 3 tablespoons of the soup and mix it with the sour cream to create a smooth paste. Stir it into the pot with a whisk, without bringing the soup back to a boil. Serve hot. This soup will keep for two days in the fridge.

NOTE
Never wash mushrooms under running water – always wipe them with a damp paper towel. If using button mushrooms, trim the stems to about ½ inch below the cap.

Fleisch und Fische

MEAT AND FISH

Meat has always played a significant role in Viennese cuisine. The Austro-Hungarian Monarchy or Empire, which formed in 1867 and lasted until 1918, spanned modern-day Austria, Hungary, Bohemia, Moravia, Slovakia, and parts of Poland, Romania, Slovenia, Croatia, and Italy. Vienna was one of the two capital cities of the Monarchy and the dishes influenced by these many cultures made their way to Hertha's cookbook and continue to remain at the heart of Viennese cooking today. *Szegediner Goulash* (see page 58), originating from Hungary; the famed *Wiener Schnitzel* (see page 61), widely believed to have stemmed from Italy in the 15th or 16th century; and fish dishes named Yugoslavian Fish and Tuna Fish *Brodetto* (meaning "little broth" in Italian), taste divine and are reminders of a flavorful, culturally-rich past.

Founded in 1848, the St. Marx slaughterhouse in the center of Vienna received livestock — primarily pork and beef — from Hungary and Serbia. By the time it reached the butcher, standing orders from upper-class households were in place, with servants regularly fetching the orders for the next few days. A beef bouillon would be prepared almost daily, simmering on the stove from early morning.

Arabisches Reiterfleisch

ARABIAN MEATLOAF

SERVES 2-3

5 oz ground beef

½ medium onion, peeled and
very finely chopped

1 small pickle, finely chopped

2 small apples, peeled, cored,
and cut into tiny cubes

2 tsp grated fresh horseradish

3 tsp tomato paste

Salt and freshly ground
pepper

Paprika

1 tsp sugar

1 large egg

2 tbsp butter

Scant ¼ cup sour cream

Preheat to the oven to 350°F/190°C.

Mix all the ingredients together in a bowl, except for the butter and the sour cream.

Melt the butter over medium to high heat in a 10-inch cast-iron ovensafe frying pan until it begins to bubble (but not brown), then remove from heat. A frying pan gives a better result as the edges of the meatloaf become crusty and more flavorful.

Place the mixture into the hot butter and pat it down so that it is evenly distributed in the pan. Transfer the pan to the preheated oven and bake for 35 to 40 minutes, until it is nicely browned. Remove from the oven, pour the sour cream over the top, and cook for another 5 minutes. Despite its exotic name, this is a simple, almost rustic dish, nicely complemented with rice and a green salad.

Literally translated, *Arabisches Reiterfleisch* means "Arabian horseman's meat." It was a dish invented and popularized in the 1950s by Germany's first TV chef, Clemens Wilmenrod. Tante Hertha was likely not a regular TV watcher in 1953 when the program first aired, but nevertheless, the recipe charmingly found its way into her cookbook.

Gerollte Rindschnitzel
ROLLED BEEFSTEAK

**SERVES 6
(MAKES 8 ROLLS)**

2¼ lb boneless sirloin or
rib-eye steak, cut into ½-inch
slices at the butcher

**Salt and freshly ground
pepper**

2 oz spicy pork sausage meat

2 oz "lardo di colonnata"
(streaky bacon will do)

2 oz pickles

4 tbsp/2 oz butter

⅓ cup light corn oil

1 medium onion, peeled
and finely chopped

2 tbsp flour

1 cup sour cream

Pound the meat with a tenderizer until very thin. Score each slice at the edges. Season each side liberally with salt and pepper. Now spread a thin layer of sausage meat (squeezing it out of the casing) on top of each piece, as if you were buttering bread.

Cut the bacon and pickles into thin strips. Place a few strips of bacon and pickles lengthwise at the base of each slice of meat and roll up tightly, securing both ends with string so that the rolls hold their shape.

Heat the butter and oil in a frying pan over medium to high heat, making sure the fat does not start to smoke. Add as many rolls as will fit in the pan and brown evenly on all sides. When all the pieces have been browned, transfer them to a large saucepan and set aside.

Turn the heat down a little and add the onion to the frying pan (you may need to add a little more fat) and fry to a rich golden color. Now add enough cold water to just barely cover the onions. As soon as they are brought to a boil, pour the onions and water over the meat rolls in the saucepan. Cover with a lid and simmer on low heat for 45 minutes to 1 hour, until the meat is tender. Check periodically, and if necessary, add small quantities of water. The meat should be braising in its own juice so be sure to add water very sparingly. When cooked, remove the rolls from the pan (but reserve the juice) and arrange them on a serving platter. Keep warm in a low oven while preparing the gravy.

To make the gravy, mix the flour with the sour cream, add it to the reserved pan juices, and bring to a gentle boil, stirring all the time. Reduce the heat and continue stirring regularly for another 10–15 minutes. If the sauce becomes too thick, add a little more water so that the consistency is more like a gravy rather than a thick béchamel-style sauce. Remove from the heat. Strain the sauce through a sieve into a bowl, pressing the sauce through the strainer with the back of a metal spoon. Season to taste.

Remove the meat rolls from the oven and pour some of the sauce over them and the rest into a saucière for the dinner table. Serve with boiled new potatoes or *Semmelknödeln* (see page 94), a typical Austrian dumpling.

Szegediner Gulyás
SZEGEDINER GOULASH

SERVES 6

2¼ lb sauerkraut

¼ lb smoked speck (cured fatty bacon) or pancetta

1 tsp sunflower oil

4 medium onions, peeled and finely chopped

1 tbsp paprika

1 heaped tsp caraway seeds

Salt

A little chicken stock

½ green pepper, cut into thin strips

2¼ lb pork shoulder or belly

2 tbsp lard or butter

1 clove of garlic, peeled and crushed

1 tbsp paprika

½ tomato, chopped

½ tsp black peppercorns

2 tsp all-purpose flour

½ cup sour cream

Drain the liquid from the sauerkraut and reserve the juice.

Cut the smoked speck into ½-inch cubes. Heat the oil in a heavy-base casserole dish and gently fry the speck or pancetta on medium heat. Add two of the onions and fry until golden. Remove from heat, add the paprika and caraway seeds, stir, and return to the heat, adding the drained sauerkraut with a pinch of salt. Add a little chicken stock so that it just covers the bottom of the casserole dish. Cover and simmer over low heat for approximately 50 minutes. During this time, check that the dish hasn't dried out (if it's looking a little dry, add a little more chicken stock but make sure there isn't too much liquid), then add the green pepper strips and cook for another 10 minutes.

Meanwhile, cut the pork into 1-inch cubes and season with salt. In a separate heavy-base casserole dish, melt the lard or butter and gently fry the remaining two onions until softened and then add the garlic. Reduce the heat, add the paprika, then add the pork and season with salt. Brown in batches rather than all at once. Return all the meat to the casserole dish and add the tomato, peppercorns, and just enough water or chicken stock to prevent burning. Reduce the heat to very low, stir in the flour to coat the meat, and simmer for about 1 hour, until the meat is tender. Add a little more water or chicken stock only if absolutely necessary: the less additional liquid added the better, so that the meat is essentially swimming in its own juices.

Now combine the sauerkraut with the meat and stir lightly. Add the sour cream before serving, making sure not to mix it in completely: a few streaks of sour cream should remain.

NOTE

If pressed for time, you can prepare the first step of the recipe a day in advance. The flavors improve over time with this dish, making any leftovers even more tasty. If reheating, warm on a gentle heat without letting it come to a boil.

Wiener Schnitzel

WIENER SCHNITZEL

SERVES 4

½ cup all-purpose flour

2 large eggs, lightly beaten

4 oz breadcrumbs

4 × 5-oz veal cutlets (you could also use pork or chicken fillets)

1 tsp salt

Lard or oil, for frying

Lemon wedges, to serve

You will need three plates: place the flour in the first, the lightly beaten eggs in the second, and the breadcrumbs in the third.

Pound each cutlet with a meat tenderizer to a thickness of ¼-inch. With a sharp knife, make small cuts every 1 inch around the edges of the meat; this ensures that the meat will stay flat and not curl up when frying. Season both sides with salt and set aside.

Coat both sides of each cutlet first in the flour, then in the egg, and lastly in the breadcrumbs. When turning the cutlets over in the breadcrumbs, do not pat down the crumbs or the crispiness of the coating will be lost in the frying process.

The best and most authentic taste for frying is lard, but any oil (except olive oil) can be used instead. Heat the lard or oil in a frying pan on medium high heat and fry the cutlets for 2–3 minutes on each side until golden, gently shaking the pan. Make sure there is always enough fat in the pan so that the cutlets do not stick to the surface. Remove and drain on paper towels.

This dish is always served with a wedge of lemon alongside. A cucumber salad and/or potato salad are traditional and delicious accompaniments.

Though synonymous with the idea of Viennese cuisine, Tante Hertha did not have this dish in her cookbook. For *Wiener Schnitzel*, one would go to the local *Wirtshaus*, a kind of countrified pub where simple but delicious fresh dishes are served. Every Austrian knows how to prepare this specialty by heart, which likely explains the absence of a documented recipe. Nonetheless, it remains a must-have in the Viennese repertoire so we are including it, by heart, here.

Wurzelfleisch
Sharon Schauenstein

PORK ROAST WITH ROOT VEGETABLES

SERVES 4

2¼ lb pork shoulder

1 tsp salt

1 tsp caraway seeds

1 glove of garlic, peeled
and chopped

2 tbsp corn oil

¼ lb carrots, peeled and finely
sliced

¼ lb celeriac, peeled and
cut into ¼-inch slices

¼ lb parsley root, peeled
and cut into ¼-inch slices

¼ lb parsnips, peeled and
finely sliced

Onion, peeled and cut into
¼-inch slices

Preheat to the oven to 325°F/160°C.

In a small bowl, mix the salt with the caraway seeds and garlic into a paste and rub into the surface of the meat.

In a frying pan, heat the oil and sear the meat on all sides for 2–3 minutes until lightly browned. Now transfer the meat to a roasting pan. Cook for 1 hour, basting the meat with its own juices from time to time.

After 1 hour, turn the meat and arrange the prepared vegetables around the roast. Cook for another 1–1½ hours. During this time, check that the meat isn't drying out by adding small amounts of water if necessary (it should not be swimming in liquid though). You will end up with colorfully glazed vegetables and a tender, tasty meat dish.

To serve, transfer the meat and vegetables to a warmed serving dish and cut into thin slices. For a hearty meal, *Semmelknödeln* (see page 94) can also be served as a side dish.

Fisch im Bierteig

BEER-BATTERED FISH

SERVES 6

FOR THE FISH

6 x 5-oz white fish fillets of your choice (such as cod or haddock)

Salt

Juice of 1 lemon

FOR THE BATTER

1½ cups/6½ oz all-purpose flour

1 tsp salt

¾ cup beer

1 tbsp oil

2 large egg yolks

2–3 large egg whites

Light vegetable oil, for frying

Lemon wedges, to garnish

Season the fish pieces on both sides with salt and sprinkle sparingly with the lemon juice.

To make the batter, beat the flour, salt, beer, oil, and egg yolks together in a bowl to a smooth batter using an electric mixer. Set the batter aside to rest for 30 minutes.

Just before the 30 minutes are up, whisk the egg whites until stiff. Fold them swiftly and gently into the beer batter.

Heat the oil in a large heavy-base pan or deep fryer until a cube of stale bread turns golden in 30 seconds. Reduce the heat a little, then dip the fish into the batter and fry in the hot oil on both sides until golden brown. Drain on paper towels. Serve with new potatoes in butter and freshly chopped flat-leaf parsley.

Jugoslawischer Fisch
YUGOSLAVIAN FISH

SERVES 2–3

1¼ lb white fish fillet of your choice (such as cod, haddock, or trout), cut into large chunks

1 large onion, peeled and very finely chopped

1 clove of garlic, peeled and crushed

3½ oz tomato paste

Scant cup whipping cream

Salt

½ tsp peppercorns

1 tsp paprika

1 large egg yolk

Gewürze nach Geschmack (this translates as 'seasoning of your choice'. Tante Hertha wasn't specific, so use your favorite spices to complement the fish, such as light paprika, tarragon, thyme, or freshly chopped flat-leaf parsley)

3 tbsp cold butter, plus extra for greasing

1 oz freshly grated Parmesan cheese

Preheat to the oven to 375°F/190°C.

In a bowl, mix the fish and all the other ingredients together, (minus the cold butter and cheese).

Generously butter an ovensafe baking dish and pour in the fish mixture. Sprinkle a liberal amount of grated Parmesan cheese over the top. Top off with shavings of butter (make sure the butter is really cold). Bake for 20–25 minutes until golden. Serve with boiled rice.

Hausgemachte Mayonnaise

HOMEMADE MAYONNAISE

MAKES ⅔ CUP

2 large egg yolks

½ tsp salt

½ cup sunflower oil

2 tsp fresh lemon juice,
to taste

½ tsp Worcestershire sauce

½–1 tsp Dijon mustard, or
to taste

Few drops of Tabasco sauce

Pinch of sugar

Pinch of cayenne pepper

Freshly ground white pepper

Put the egg yolks in a mixing bowl with the salt. Place a folded damp kitchen cloth underneath the bowl to prevent it from sliding.

Using a medium-size balloon whisk, whisk the egg yolks. To begin with, add the oil drop by drop, whisking all the time (you can use a turkey baster to ensure the oil is added slowly). The drop-by-drop approach will provide the right texture so that the mayonnaise is firm and not too runny.

As the consistency begins to thicken, you can add the oil in a thin trickle, whisking all the time. Stop every now and then in between each trickle to make sure the oil is properly incorporated. Once the texture becomes quite thick and you have used half the oil, whisk in the lemon juice. Trickle in the remaining oil until it is all incorporated. Using a spoon, mix in the Worcestershire sauce, mustard, Tabasco sauce, sugar, cayenne pepper, and pepper, to taste. Transfer to a clean, airtight glass jar. Keep refrigerated for up to one week.

NOTE
Keep all ingredients and utensils at room temperature. A cold bowl will prevent the mayonnaise from thickening.

Kräutersauce

HERB SAUCE

MAKES ABOUT ⅓ CUP

FOR THE MAYONNAISE
1 large egg yolk
⅓ cup sunflower oil
2–3 tsp lemon juice
Freshly ground pepper
Pinch of mild curry powder
½ tsp superfine sugar
Dash of Worcestershire sauce

FOR THE ANCHOVY PASTE
2 anchovy fillets, finely chopped
1 tsp Dijon mustard
1 liberal handful of baby spinach
Half a handful of flat-leaf parsley
Half a handful of dill
Half a handful of chives
Half a handful of lemon thyme
2–3 mint leaves
1 tsp coarsely chopped capers
2–3 tsp sour cream

Start by making the mayonnaise. Using a medium-size balloon whisk, whisk the egg yolk. To begin with, add the oil drop by drop, whisking all the time (you can use a turkey baster to ensure the oil is added slowly). The drop-by-drop approach will provide the right texture so that the mayonnaise is firm and not too runny.

As the consistency begins to thicken, you can add the oil in a thin trickle, whisking all the time. Stop every now and then in between each trickle to make sure the oil is properly incorporated. Once the texture becomes quite thick and you have used half the oil, whisk in the lemon juice. Trickle in the remaining oil until it is all incorporated. Using a spoon, mix in a grinding of pepper, the curry powder, sugar, and Worcestershire sauce. Set aside.

Now make the anchovy paste. In a separate small bowl, mash the anchovies into a smooth paste with the back of a spoon and then stir into the mayonnaise (canned anchovies taste much better than ready-made anchovy paste, so avoid this shortcut). Mix in the mustard.

Pulse the spinach and all the herbs in a food processor until smooth but not quite a paste. Add the capers and pulse to a paste.

Place a sieve over the bowl of mayonnaise and transfer the herb paste to the sieve. Press the paste through the sieve with the back of a metal spoon, turning it a lovely pale green color. Stop halfway through to stir the herb juices into the mayonnaise to make sure that the mayonnaise is not becoming too runny. The end result should be a fairly thick sauce, just like mayonnaise. Adjust the seasoning, if necessary, and finally mix in the sour cream. Transfer to a clean, airtight glass jar. Keep refrigerated for up to five days.

This sauce is delicious served with fish and fried meats and is particularly good with pan-fried wild trout.

Sardellensauce
ANCHOVY SAUCE

MAKES ⅔ CUP

½ cup oil (use the oil from the anchovies and top up with sunflower oil)

6 canned anchovies, finely chopped

1 tbsp capers, finely chopped

2 heaped tbsp very finely chopped flat-leaf parsley

1–2 tsp lemon juice

Heat 3 tablespoons of the oil in a saucepan over medium heat. Add the chopped anchovies and stir until the anchovies form a smooth paste. Add the remaining oil and heat until it bubbles. Mix in the capers and parsley, and 1 teaspoon of the lemon juice. Add the second teaspoon cautiously, according to taste. Remove from the heat.

This sauce makes a perfect accompaniment to roast meat.

Schnittlauchsauce

CHIVE SAUCE

MAKES 1¼ CUP

2 stale white bread rolls

Vinegar water (6 tbsp water to 3 tbsp mild white wine vinegar)

2 large egg yolks

½ tsp salt

½ cup oil (half sunflower oil and half light olive oil)

1–2 tsp lemon juice, to taste (use more than 1 tsp if necessary)

6 tbsp finely chopped chives

Dash or two of Worcestershire sauce

1 tsp or more Dijon mustard, to taste

Few drops of Tabasco sauce

½ tsp sugar

Freshly ground pepper

3 medium hard-boiled eggs, roughly chopped

4 tbsp sour cream

Use a grater to remove the crusts from the rolls. Cut the dough into ½-inch cubes. Pour the vinegar water over the bread, cover, and marinate for about 15 minutes.

Put the egg yolks in a mixing bowl with the salt. Place a folded damp kitchen cloth underneath the bowl to prevent it from sliding.

Using a medium-size balloon whisk, whisk the egg yolks. To begin with, add the oil drop by drop, whisking all the time (you can use a turkey baster to ensure the oil is added slowly). The drop-by-drop approach will provide the right texture so that the mayonnaise is firm and not too runny.

As the consistency begins to thicken, you can add the oil in a thin trickle, whisking all the time. Stop every now and then in between each trickle to make sure the oil is properly incorporated. Once the texture becomes quite thick (and you have used half the oil), whisk in the lemon juice. You can then trickle in the remaining oil until it is all incorporated. Using a spoon, mix in the chives, along with Worcestershire sauce, mustard, Tabasco sauce, sugar, and pepper, to taste. Set aside.

Squeeze any excess liquid out of the bread. In a food processor, add the bread along with the chopped hard-boiled eggs and pulse until puréed. Mix the puréed bread mixture into the mayonnaise with the sour cream. Transfer to a clean, airtight glass jar. Keep refrigerated for up to one week.

Classically served with *Rindfleisch* (boiled beef), it also serves as a wonderful complement to any white fish.

Gesalzene Mehlspeisen

MAINS

Gesalzene Mehlspeisen have a place all of their own in any Austrian cookbook or menu. These savory, primarily meat-free dishes are not prepared for formal occasions but rather as a light lunch or dinner, or on a given Friday when meat was traditionally not eaten. Because of their less formal nature, these all-in-one dishes are served among family or close friends only. Some favorite recipes however, such as *Heidensterz* (see page 75), take a certain amount of skill to prepare to perfection and because of this, have risen to an elevated status as dishes requested for special occasions, perhaps during a family ski vacation or by a young student returning home for break.

In grander times, landowners' daughters would have been sent to finishing school so they could teach the cooks — often girls from small villages — how to make these beloved dishes. The regional dishes were ones the girls would have likely already known, having inherited the recipes from their own mothers on the farms. Now as then, a local *Gasthaus* (tavern) offers such specialties, with regional favorites varying across the nine provinces of Austria.

Gemüseauflauf

MIXED VEGETABLE SOUFFLÉ

SERVES 4

FOR THE VEGETABLES

5 oz fresh green peas

½ lb Brussels sprouts, halved

½ head cauliflower, cut into small rosettes

Scant ¼ lb carrots, peeled and cubed

2 oz mushrooms of your choice (chanterelles are best), sliced

1½ tbsp butter

FOR THE BÉCHAMEL

4 tbsp/2 oz butter

½ cup/2 oz all-purpose flour

1½ cups whole milk, warmed

Salt

4 large eggs, separated

Butter, for greasing

Preheat the oven to 350°F/180°C.

Start by preparing the vegetables. Boil all the vegetables (except the mushrooms) in salted water until tender, then drain. Heat the butter in a saucepan and fry the mushrooms, uncovered, stirring regularly until all the liquid has evaporated, then remove from the heat. Set aside the vegetables and prepare the béchamel.

To make the béchamel, melt the butter in a saucepan over medium heat. Stir in the flour, which will be quickly absorbed by the butter. Pour in the warmed milk gradually, stirring all the time, until all the milk has been used and the mixture comes to a light boil; this should take about 5 minutes. When the sauce appears smooth, lower the heat and season with salt. Cook for another 2 minutes, stirring continuously but with less vigor. This should result in a fairly thick, smooth sauce. Remove from heat and set aside to cool.

Once cooled, stir the egg yolks and the prepared vegetables into the béchamel. In a separate clean bowl, whisk the egg whites until they form stiff peaks, then gently fold them into the vegetable and sauce mixture. Transfer into a greased ovensafe casserole dish and bake, uncovered, for 45 minutes. Serve with a tomato salad.

Heidensterz

BUCKWHEAT CRUMBLE

SERVES 4

Generous 2 cups organic buckwheat flour

½ tsp salt

5½ tbsp/2½ oz lard or butter (the authentic recipes use lard)

In a large frying pan on low heat, dry-roast the buckwheat flour for about 10 minutes, stirring gently, until all the moisture has evaporated.

In a saucepan, bring 1¼ cups water to a boil with the salt. Add the roasted buckwheat flour to the pan all at once. Cover and reduce the heat to low, and steep for about 10 minutes.

In the meantime, heat the lard or butter in a large, deep saucepan until it begins to bubble. Remove from the heat, then stir it into the buckwheat using a wooden spoon. Cover and allow to set in the pan, until ready to serve. Though known throughout Austria, this dish is traditionally served in the provinces of Styria and Carinthia, with a sauce of freshly picked wild mushrooms.

Herrentorte
GENTLEMAN'S TORTE

SERVES 6

FOR THE BASE

14 tbsp/7 oz butter, plus extra for greasing

1 large egg

Generous ½ lb curd cheese (or Austrian *Topfen* if available), pushed through a sieve

2½ cups/10½ oz all-purpose flour, sifted, plus extra for flouring

1 tsp baking powder, sifted

1 tsp salt

FOR THE FILLING

7 tbsp/3½ oz butter

¼ lb Camembert cheese, cut into small chunks

Generous 1 lb curd cheese, pushed through a sieve

1 tsp fresh horseradish, grated

1 tsp sugar

2 tbsp finely chopped chives

Salt and freshly ground pepper

2 tbsp finely chopped flat-leaf parsley

5 oz black forest ham, chopped

FOR THE TOPPING AND DECORATION

1 slice of pumpernickel bread (optional)

A few slices of salami

3 medium hard-boiled eggs, sliced

A few green olives

A few radishes

Curly parsley, to garnish

Preheat the oven to 375°F/190°C.

Start by making the base. In a bowl, beat the butter until light and fluffy using an electric mixer. Beat in the egg, then stir in the curd cheese, followed by the sifted flour and baking powder, and salt. Cover the dough with plastic wrap and set aside to rest for 1 hour in the fridge. Remove from the fridge 10 minutes before rolling, so that the dough is not too hard.

Sprinkle a little flour over a work surface, divide the dough into three equal portions, and roll each into an 8-inch disc. Line a baking sheet with parchment paper and butter very lightly. Bake in middle rack of the oven for 25 minutes. Remove from the oven and transfer onto cooling racks until ready to use.

To make the filling, whisk the butter in a bowl using an electric mixer on a low speed until light and fluffy. Whisk in the Camembert. Now stir in the curd cheese, horseradish, and sugar, and season with salt and pepper. Divide the mixture into two equal portions. In one half, stir in the parsley and the chopped ham.

Place the first disc on a tray and spread half the ham-based mixture over it. Place the second disc on top and spread the remaining half of the ham-based filling. Top with the final disc. Spread the plain mixture over the top and sides, just like you would ice a cake.

Crumble the pumpernickel between your fingers and sprinkle over the top of the torte. Not everyone likes pumpernickel, so leave it out if you prefer. Decorate to your heart's content with slices of salami, hard-boiled eggs, olives, and radishes. Garnish with a few sprigs of curly parsley.

Palatschinken mit gesalzener Füllung

SAVORY CRÊPES

MAKES 12

FOR THE CRÊPES

1¼ cups/5 oz all-purpose flour

1 cup milk (or ½ milk and ½ heavy cream)

2 large eggs

2 large egg yolks

¼ tsp salt

4 tbsp/2 oz butter, for frying

Put the flour in a mixing bowl and slowly add the milk, then the whole eggs, followed by the yolks, and the salt, whisking with a balloon whisk between each addition, to a smooth thin batter. Melt a knob of butter in a medium-size frying pan over medium to high heat, tilting the pan so that it is evenly coated in butter. Pour a small ladleful of batter into the pan and tilt quickly so that the batter thinly covers the surface of the pan and is evenly distributed. Cook for about a minute, or until the crêpe is light golden. Carefully flip over and cook on the other side (the other side will cook much more quickly).

Stack the crêpes on top of each other on a warmed plate and keep in a warm oven. Fill each crêpe with your filling of choice.

HERB FILLING (ENOUGH FOR 12 CRÊPES)

5 oz quark (or Austrian *Topfen* if available)

½ cup plain yogurt

Pinch of salt, dried thyme, and basil

7 oz smoked ham, very finely chopped

Butter, for greasing

7 oz tomatoes, skinned, seeded and cut into small cubes

Heaped tbsp grated Parmesan or other hard cheese of choice

In a bowl, mix the quark, yogurt, salt, herbs, and ham together. Spread each crêpe with the filling. Fold in half or like an envelope and place in a buttered ovensafe dish. Sprinkle over the cubed tomatoes and top with the Parmesan. Cook in a preheated 400°F/200°C oven for 10 to 15 minutes.

NOTE
The first crêpe is usually not a "masterpiece" and should be eaten by the cook. By the time you come to make the second crêpe, the pan will be at the optimum temperature and all subsequent crêpe will be just so.

MUSHROOM FILLING (ENOUGH FOR 12 CRÊPES)

1½ tbsp/¼ oz butter

½ medium onion, peeled and finely chopped

2 heaped tbsp finely chopped flat-leaf parsley

7 oz button or fresh wild mushrooms, wiped clean and finely chopped

Salt and freshly ground pepper

1–2 tbsp crème fraîche (optional)

Melt the butter in a heavy-based frying pan over medium to high heat until it begins to bubble. Fry the onion until translucent, then add the parsley and the mushrooms. When all begins to bubble, reduce the heat to medium-low and cook until all the moisture has evaporated. Remove from the heat and season with salt and pepper. If using, add the crème fraîche gradually and make sure the filling isn't too runny.

Spread each crêpe with the filling, roll up, then place them in an ovensafe dish and keep them warm in a preheated 275°F/140°C oven until they are ready to serve. Alternatively, instead of rolling the crêpes, place the filling into the center of each crêpe, then fold over like an envelope.

Lachsfleckerln
BAKED NOODLES WITH SALMON

SERVES 4

Butter, for greasing

1½ tbsp fine breadcrumbs

7 oz extra-broad egg noodles
(or *Fleckerln* if available)

¾ lb poached boned salmon

5 tbsp/2½ oz butter, at room
temperature

4 large eggs, separated

½ cup sour cream

Salt and freshly ground
pepper

Preheat to the oven to 350°F/180°C.

Grease a 9-inch square baking dish with butter and sprinkle with the breadcrumbs, then tip out the excess breadcrumbs.

Break the noodles in half and boil in salted water for 7–10 minutes, until al dente, then drain. In the meantime, coarsely chop the salmon in a food processor and set aside.

In the bowl of an electric mixer, cream the butter until light and fluffy, then add the egg yolks, one at a time, beating thoroughly after each addition. Stir in the sour cream and the salmon. Season with salt and pepper.

In a clean bowl, whisk the egg whites to stiff peaks.

Mix the noodles into the creamed mixture and fold in the egg whites. Transfer to the baking dish and bake for 35–40 minutes. Serve with a green salad.

NOTE
Square egg noodles (or *Fleckerln*) can be purchased in kosher delicatessens. Otherwise, standard egg noodles are a fine substitute.

Slawonischer Strudel

STRUDEL-LIKE BRIOCHE

SERVES 4

1 oz fresh yeast

2 tsp sugar

1 cup lukewarm milk

Scant 4 cups/17½ oz white bread flour, plus extra for flouring

1½ tsp salt

3–4 egg yolks, depending on size

7 tbsp/3½ oz butter, melted

Sunflower oil, for greasing

10½ tbsp/5 oz butter

Note: All ingredients should be at room temperature.

YEAST EQUIVALENTS

1 tbsp/¼ oz of dry yeast is equivalent to 2 tbsp/½ oz of compressed or fresh yeast. Dry yeast doesn't dissolve well in milk, so dissolve it in a little warm water first, before adding the milk called for in the recipe.

In a warmed mixing bowl, cream the yeast with the sugar, add 5 tablespoons of the lukewarm milk, and mix until smooth. Move to a warm place to rise (either a sunny spot or an oven preheated to its lowest setting and then turned off) for 10–15 minutes, or until the mixture is halfway up the bowl.

Sift the flour onto a clean work surface and add the salt. Make a large well in the center and drop 3 egg yolks into the well. Add the raised yeast, drawing in the flour from the edges with your fingertips or a pastry scraper, and add the melted butter with the remainder of the milk. Gently work the dough until it is soft and slightly sticky; add another egg yolk if necessary.

Knead the dough, scraping the work surface with the pastry scraper. Sprinkle a little extra flour around the dough so that it does not stick to the surface. Develop a rhythmic action and knead for between 10 and 15 minutes until soft and even-textured. The dough should be very elastic, soft, and satiny-smooth.

Shape the dough into a ball. Place it into a warmed bowl lightly greased with oil, and turn the dough over so that it is evenly coated in oil. Cover with a damp dish towel and set aside to rise in a warm, draft-free place, for about 1–1½ hours.

When almost doubled in size, punch the dough down to its original size, then roll it out into a 12- x 16-inch rectangle.

Meanwhile beat the butter in a bowl using an electric mixer until light and fluffy. Spread the whipped butter over the dough, leaving a ¾-inch clear border all round. Roll the rectangle into a cylinder, pressing down the seam to seal it.

Transfer the strudel onto a baking sheet, seam-down. Press down the ends of the roll to seal. Cover with a dry dish towel and set aside to rise once again in a warm place, for 30–35 minutes, until almost doubled in size. Preheat oven to 400°F/200°C. Bake for 25–35 minutes until golden in color and hollow in sound when tapped on the surface. Serve with a green salad or a herring and potato salad.

Spinatroulade

SPINACH ROULADE

SERVES 4

FOR THE PASTRY

1 lb spinach leaves

3 tbsp/1½ oz butter, plus extra for greasing

⅓ cup all-purpose flour

½ cup milk

Salt and freshly ground pepper

4 large eggs, separated

FOR THE FILLING

1 tbsp butter

1 tbsp all-purpose flour

½ cup milk

Salt

5 oz ham, very finely chopped

Grated Parmesan cheese, to serve

AN INDULGENT OPTION…

Tante Hertha used to pour melted butter over the warm roulade. Cholesterol wasn't even in the picture back then!

Preheat the oven to 375°F/190°C. Line a baking sheet with parchment paper, then lightly grease it and dust it with flour.

Start by making the dough. Thoroughly wash the spinach, drain the excess water and cook in a covered pan on gentle heat until wilted. Drain and when cool enough to handle, use your hands to squeeze out the remaining water. Purée the spinach in a food processor and set aside.

Melt the butter in a heavy-base saucepan. Whisk in the flour and cook until bubbling, for about a minute. Remove the pan from the heat and let it cool slightly, before gradually adding in the milk, whisking all the time. Return to the heat, bring to a boil, and whisk constantly until thick and the sauce comes away from the sides of the pan. Remove from the heat and season with salt and pepper. Mix in the spinach, transfer to a large bowl, and set aside to cool, then fold the egg yolks into the mixture, one at a time.

In a separate clean bowl, whisk the egg whites into stiff peaks using an electric mixer. Using a spatula, gently fold the egg whites into the cooled spinach mixture. Spread the mixture evenly into the prepared baking sheet and bake for 10–15 minutes, making sure a crust does not form, then remove from the oven.

Meanwhile, prepare the filling. In a saucepan, melt the butter over medium heat, then add the flour, stirring all the while, until the mixture begins to bubble. Remove from the heat and, while stirring vigorously with a wooden spoon, slowly add just enough milk to thicken. Return to the heat and continue to add the milk cautiously, stirring all the while, to prevent lumps from forming. The sauce should be of a medium thickness. Season with a little salt if necessary (the ham may be sufficiently salty). Simmer for another 2 minutes, then stir in the ham.

Carefully tip the pastry onto a clean dish towel, parchment side-up. Gently peel off the paper, then with the pastry still on the dish towel, roll and unroll the pastry twice (the pastry is pliable enough to do this without cracking) to "train" it into shape. Spread the filling evenly over the surface using a spatula. Using the dish towel underneath to guide you, carefully roll the filled pastry as tightly as possible. Ease the roll onto a warmed serving dish, seam-side down. Sprinkle with Parmesan and serve immediately.

Beilagen, Salate und Gemüse

SIDES, SALADS, AND VEGETABLES

The Naschmarkt is Vienna's central outdoor market. Established in the 16th century, it mainly sold bottled milk. From 1793 onwards, all fruits and vegetables brought to Vienna by land had to be sold here, while goods arriving from the Danube were sold elsewhere. Ash (or *Asch*), from which milk bottles were made, led to the name Aschenmarkt. *Naschen* means "to nibble or graze," so the evolvement of its name to Naschmarkt by 1820 seems very fitting.

A walk to the Naschmarkt from Hertha's centrally located apartment took about 30 minutes. Hertha would have made her way down the fashionable Kärtner Straße, with its fine jewelers and exquisite boutiques, bypassing her beloved opera house and turning onto the Ring, its colorful red trams circling the inner city and beyond. Hertha's basket was filled almost daily with the fresh produce on offer – root vegetables, potatoes, cabbage for sauerkraut, cucumbers – all those most favored in Viennese cuisine.

A standard *Beilage* (side dish) includes a type of bready dumpling. Usually accompanying a gravy-based meat dish, these dumplings are equally good on their own with a freshly made sauce and flavored with parsley.

Erdäpfelkren

HORSERADISH MASH

SERVES 4

1 lb mashing potatoes
(such as Desiree or Romano)

½ cup mayonnaise
(see page 68)

Scant ⅓ cup lukewarm milk

1 tsp lemon juice

Dash of tarragon vinegar
(optional)

2–3 tbsp finely grated
horseradish

Salt

Boil the potatoes in their skins until tender. Drain and peel when cool enough to handle. Cut the potatoes into chunks and press them through a potato ricer into a mixing bowl.

Add the mayonnaise and milk in alternates, one tablespoon at a time, until you achieve a creamy mash consistency. Add the lemon juice and a dash of vinegar, if using. Finally, add the horseradish and season with salt.

Perfect with grilled meat dishes or sausages.

Gebackenes Sauerkraut

BAKED SAUERKRAUT

SERVES 4

1½ oz streaky bacon

1 scant tablespoon sugar

1 medium-small onion, peeled and finely chopped

1½ lb sauerkraut, rinsed and drained

Salt

2¼ lb floury potatoes

3 tbsp lard or sunflower oil, plus extra for greasing

5–7 oz sausage of your choice (Polish kielbassa, or cured ham)

2 large eggs, hard-boiled and sliced

½–⅔ cup sour cream

Preheat the oven to 350°F/180°C.

Cut the bacon into small cubes and gently fry it in its own fat until it begins to color. Add the sugar and the onion and fry until the onion becomes translucent and is just starting to turn a golden color.

Add the sauerkraut to the pan (the rinsing process can be omitted altogether — leave unrinsed for a tangier, slightly more acidic taste), season with a pinch of salt and cover. Turn up the heat until the contents come to a boil, then reduce to a simmer for 30 minutes, until the sauerkraut is tender. If the liquid looks like it is drying up, add a few teaspoons of water, but only add the water if absolutely necessary as it is best if the sauerkraut tenderizes in its own juices.

Meanwhile, steam the potatoes in their skins until tender. When cooled, peel and thinly slice them. Fry the slices in the lard or oil with a pinch of salt to dry them out and get rid of any excess water.

Lightly grease a 9-inch square, 1-inch deep ovensafe dish. Slice the sausages or ham (or a combination of both). Cover the bottom of the dish with half the fried potatoes, then add a layer of sauerkraut, then a layer of sliced sausages or ham. Cover with the sliced eggs and the remainder of the potatoes. Top with the sour cream, making sure to cover the entire surface. Bake uncovered for approximately 30–35 minutes. Serve with a mixed green salad.

Heringssalat

HERRING SALAD

SERVES 4

3⅓ lb Jersey Royal or similar waxy potatoes

5 oz carrots, peeled

5 oz pickles

5 oz green beans

7–9 oz herring in oil or Matjes herring fillets

1 tbsp capers, finely chopped

½ lb Bramley or similar cooking apples, peeled and cubed

⅓ cup, or slightly less, olive oil

Dash of white wine vinegar

1 tsp Dijon mustard

½ cup sour cream

Salt and freshly ground pepper

Steam the potatoes in their skins with the whole carrots until tender. When cooled, peel the potatoes and cube them. Cut the carrots and pickles into small cubes.

Boil the green beans for a couple of minutes until just tender. Drain and run under cold water, then slice them into ½-inch-long pieces.

Rinse the herring thoroughly, pat with paper towels to remove the excess oil, cut into small cubes, and place into a bowl. Add the potatoes, carrots, pickles, green beans, capers, and apples.

In a separate bowl mix together the oil, vinegar, mustard, and sour cream, then mix it into the herring mixture. Season with salt and pepper. Cover and marinate in the refrigerator for a few hours so that all the flavors infuse.

Remove from the refrigerator 30 minutes before serving. Serve on a mound of green lettuce, garnished with sliced hard-boiled eggs, miniature dill pickles, anchovies, and "rosettes" of homemade (see page 68) or store-bought mayonnaise.

Kartoffelmayonnaisesalat
POTATO MAYONNAISE SALAD

SERVES 4

3⅓ lb Fingerling, Jersey Royal
or similar waxy potatoes

Salt

Vinegar water (6 tbsp water
to 3 tsp light balsamic or mild
white wine vinegar)

⅔ cup homemade mayonnaise
(see page 68)

Pinch of mild curry powder

1½ oz sweet pickles, very
finely cubed

1 tbsp capers, finely chopped

2 tsp chives, snipped
(optional)

Dash of Tabasco sauce
(optional)

Boil the potatoes in their skins until tender. When cooled, peel and
thinly slice them, and sprinkle with salt. Transfer to a flat-bottomed
dish.

Pour the vinegar water over the potato slices and marinate for
no less than 1 hour, then drain any excess liquid.

In a separate bowl, mix the mayonnaise with the curry powder,
pickles, capers, and, if using, the chives and Tabasco sauce. Now
combine this mixture with the potatoes. Taste and adjust the seasoning
and spices to your personal taste. Serve with Wiener Schnitzel (see
page 61) or with any fish or grilled meat dishes.

Semmelknödeln

BREAD DUMPLINGS

SERVES 4

5 cups/½ lb stale white rolls or baguette (in Austria you can find bread specifically for dumplings called *Knödel Brot*)

1 large egg

1 large egg yolk

¾ cup milk

1½ tbsp/¾ oz butter

1 medium onion, finely chopped

1 heaped tbsp chopped flat-leaf parsley

½ tsp salt

1–2 tbsp all-purpose flour

Cut the rolls or bread into scant ½-inch cubes and place into a large bowl. In a separate bowl, beat the egg and the egg yolk with the milk and pour over the cubed bread, gently stirring with a wooden spoon to make sure all the cubes are coated with the egg mixture.

Meanwhile, heat the butter in a heavy-base frying pan over medium heat until it begins to bubble. Add the onion and fry until translucent. Mix in the parsley. Remove from the heat and pour over the bread mixture. Season with the salt and mix together with the wooden spoon, gently packing down the bread in the bowl so that it soaks up all the flavors. Set aside to absorb the liquid for 10–15 minutes. During this time, gently turn the mixture over with the spoon a couple of times, pack down again and leave to rest.

After this period, the mixture should be moist, but not dripping wet. Add 1 tablespoon of the flour, mixing it in with your hand. Feel the texture with your fingers, and if the mass holds together with a little pressure, then no more flour is needed.

Keep a bowl of warm water on hand. Wet one hand and scoop out a ball of mixture, about the size of a tennis ball. Roll into a ball, firmly pressing the mixture together so that it holds its shape. Repeat until all the mixture is used.

Bring a large pan of salted water to a boil. Carefully lower the dumplings into the pan in batches. Return to a boil, then immediately reduce the heat and simmer very gently for another 15 minutes. Use a slotted spoon to gently lift them from the pot, draining off all the water and place onto a warm plate. Keep the batches warm in a low oven.

Serve immediately with goulash or a meat dish. Any leftovers can be sliced and fried in a little butter and served as an accompaniment to wild mushroom sauce, or a green Mâche (lamb's lettuce) salad, a favorite combination of my great-grandmother's.

Warmer Krautsalat
WARM CABBAGE SALAD

SERVES 4

1 lb white cabbage

6 tbsp white wine vinegar

1 tsp salt

1 tsp sugar

1 tsp caraway seeds

¼ lb speck (cured fatty bacon), cut into ¼-inch cubes

Remove the outer leaves of the cabbage and discard. Finely shred the rest of the cabbage using a mandolin if you have one, if not a sharp knife will do – mind your fingers!

Place the shredded cabbage in a large bowl. Pour boiling water over the top and let stand a few minutes. Drain and repeat the process twice more, draining well between each scalding.

In a saucepan, mix the vinegar, salt, sugar and caraway seeds with 3 tablespoons of water and bring to a boil. Pour over the well-drained cabbage. Cover with a plate or lid to fit the bowl and allow to stand for 30 minutes.

Drain the liquid into a saucepan and bring to a boil. Remove from the heat and pour over the cabbage.

Gently fry the speck until crisp but not too browned. Remove from the heat, lifting it out with a slotted spoon, and drain on a paper towel. Transfer the cabbage onto a warmed serving dish and just before serving, sprinkle the warm bacon bits on top. Serve with roast pork or sausages.

Kürbisgemüse
CREAMED PUMPKIN

SERVES 4

1 lb 5 oz pumpkin

1 tsp salt

3 tbsp lard (or 1½ tbsp sunflower oil and 1½ tbsp butter)

½ small onion, peeled and very finely chopped

1 tsp paprika

1 tbsp white wine vinegar

1 tbsp tomato paste

1 tsp caraway seeds

½ cup sour cream

1 tsp all-purpose flour

Freshly ground pepper

Peel and seed the pumpkin and coarsely grate or shred in a food processor. Transfer to a mixing bowl and stir in the salt. Cover with plastic wrap and set aside for no less than 1 hour. Drain.

Heat the lard (or oil and butter) in a stainless steel saucepan and fry the onion on medium heat until light golden. Stir in the paprika and immediately remove the pan from the heat (paprika should not be allowed to fry for any length of time because it turns bitter). Add the vinegar and return the pan to the heat. Add the drained pumpkin together with the tomato paste and the caraway seeds. Don't be tempted to add any fluids the pumpkin will yield enough of its own juice. Mix well and cover. Bring to a rolling boil and then immediately reduce the heat and simmer for 35–40 minutes, until the pumpkin is tender. Stir a couple of times during cooking time to prevent the mixture from sticking to the bottom of the pan.

Meanwhile, mix the sour cream with the flour in a bowl. Once the pumpkin is tender, stir in the sour cream/flour mixture and gently bring it back to a gentle simmer, covered, for another 10 minutes, making sure that the heat is not too high. Adjust the seasoning if necessary and add a few grindings of pepper.

The flavor of this dish improves with time so it can be eaten up to two days after cooking. Serve with roast pork or chicken.

Serviettenknödel
DUMPLING STEAMED IN A NAPKIN

SERVES 4

FOR THE DUMPLING

11 oz day-old white rolls or white bread

2 large eggs

2 large egg yolks

2 cups milk

¼ lb speck (cured fatty bacon), cut into ¼-inch cubes

3 tbsp finely chopped flat-leaf parsley

1 tsp salt

6–8 tbsp breadcrumbs

FOR THE TOPPING

1½ tbsp/¾ oz butter

1 oz fine breadcrumbs

Cut the rolls or bread into ½-inch cubes. Place in a large bowl.

In a separate bowl, lightly beat the eggs and yolks with the milk and pour over the cubed bread. Cover and soak for 30 minutes.

Have a dish towel or cloth napkin ready, which has been soaked in cold water, wrung out, and lightly buttered on one side. Bring a large pan of salted water to a boil.

Fry the speck in its own fat on very low heat until it begins to just color. Remove from the heat and pour over the soaked bread. Using a large wooden spoon, stir in the parsley, salt, and breadcrumbs. Then use your hands to gather the mixture into one large dumpling, and place it in the center of the buttered dish towel or napkin. Gather the four corners and tie them together firmly so that the knot does not unravel, but make sure the dumpling has enough space to expand while it cooks.

Slide the handle of a long-handled wooden spoon through the ends of the napkin and gently lower the "parcel" into the pan, resting the handle along the edges of the pan so that the dumpling does not touch the bottom. Loosely cover the pan with a lid. Once the water has come to a boil again, reduce the heat and simmer gently for 45 minutes–1 hour.

Before the hour is up, prepare the breadcrumb topping. Melt the butter in a frying pan on medium to high heat until it begins to bubble. Add the breadcrumbs and stir them in the butter until they are pale golden and a little crisp.

When the dumpling is cooked, take the pan off the heat and carefully lift the dumpling from the pan. When cool enough to handle, remove the dumpling from the dish towel or napkin and transfer to a warmed plate. Sprinkle the fried breadcrumbs on top and cut into thick slices. Alternatively, it can be "torn" into small pieces shortly before being served and sprinkled with fried breadcrumbs.

Bäckereien

COOKIES, PASTRIES, AND CONFECTIONS

Most of the treats in this chapter are traditionally made for the Christmas season. Gingerbread, meringues, and chocolate truffles are hung on beautifully adorned trees on Christmas Eve. The truffles are wrapped in delicate tissue paper in a color that complements the overall decor. Red, for instance, flatters the more traditional style of tree, whereas white creates a more elegant look for gold and silver Christmas ornaments. And then there are the pastels to choose from... These tissues are either bought pre-cut or large sheets of paper are cut to size by children under the supervision of their mothers or grandmothers.

More than in any other section of Hertha's book, many names are affiliated with these recipes — aunts, cousins, and friends who would have, fittingly for the season being honored, shared their favorite recipes and made them timeless.

Having tested all of these delicacies again when writing the book, we came to the realization that it seems a shame to enjoy them for such a short season. Chocolate-laden recipes are welcome all year round, and the variety of thin wafers can be served in the summer months with ice creams and molded jello. One cookie, however, is sacred to the Christmas season: the *Vanillekipferl* (see page 136), a melt-in-your-mouth shortbread in the shape of a half-moon, dusted with homemade vanilla sugar (see page 136); it should truly remain a rarefied treat.

Butterbrölchen

BREAD-AND-BUTTER SANDWICH COOKIES

MAKES 24

FOR THE COOKIES

1⅓ cups/7 oz all-purpose flour

½ cup/4 oz superfine sugar

8½ tbsp unsalted butter

1½ oz dark (70% cocoa) chocolate, finely grated

1 oz ground hazelnuts

1 large egg

FOR THE GLAZE

¾ cup/3½ oz confectioner's sugar

2 large egg yolks

Preheat the oven to 300°F/150°C.

Start by making the cookies. Sift the flour onto a clean work surface and mix in the sugar. Chop the butter into small cubes and use your fingertips to work it into the flour and sugar until you reach a crumbly consistency. Alternatively put the flour, sugar and diced butter in a food processor and process until the mixture resembles fine breadcrumbs.

Add the grated chocolate, hazelnuts, and egg, and mix very quickly to form a dough. Divide the dough in half and roll it out into two logs about 2 inches in diameter. Wrap each log in plastic wrap and refrigerate for 1 hour.

Remove from the refrigerator and cut into ¼-inch-thick slices. Place the rounds on a baking sheet lined with parchment paper and bake for 30–35 minutes.

Remove from the oven and transfer the cookies to wire racks to cool.

In the meantime, make the glaze. In a bowl, whisk the confectioner's sugar with the egg yolks until smooth. Once cooled, spread each cookie thinly with the glaze, as you would butter a slice of bread. Store in airtight containers for a few days or in the freezer for up to three months.

Damenperletten
RAISIN SHORTCAKES

MAKES 38

4 oz raisins

3 tbsp rum

1 cup/4 oz all-purpose flour

8½ tbsp/4 oz unsalted butter, at room temperature

1 cup/4 oz confectioner's sugar

2 large egg yolks

1 tsp homemade vanilla sugar (see page 136), or ½ tsp vanilla extract

1 oz lightly toasted almonds, roughly chopped

In a small bowl, soak the raisins in the rum for 2–3 hours.

Preheat the oven to 375°F/190°C and line a baking sheet with parchment paper.

Sift the flour into a bowl. In a separate bowl, cream the butter until it is light, then whisk in the sugar until light and fluffy. Beat in one egg yolk at a time, then add the vanilla.

Using a wooden spoon, gently fold the sifted flour into the mixture, along with the soaked raisins until incorporated.

Drop one teaspoon of the batter for each cookie, spacing them well apart. Flatten the cookies with a fork dipped in cold water, and sprinkle with the chopped almonds.

Bake in batches for 20–25 minutes, until golden brown and crisp around the edges. Leave the cookies to cool on the baking sheet for about 10 minutes before peeling them off the parchment paper and transferring them to cooling racks. Allow to cool completely before storing in airtight containers for up to two weeks. Not suitable for freezing.

Gefüllte Lebkuchen

FILLED GINGERBREAD

MAKES 24

FOR THE COOKIES

⅓ cup runny honey

¼ cup/2 oz granulated sugar

½ tsp ground cinnamon

Pinch of ground cloves

Pinch of ground nutmeg

3 tbsp butter, melted and cooled

2 cups/9 oz all-purpose flour

½ tsp baking powder

1 large egg

FOR THE FILLING

2 oz ground hazelnuts

½ cup/2 oz confectioner's sugar

1 oz candied citrus peel, finely chopped

1 large egg

1 oz blanched almonds, halved, to garnish (see page 108)

1 egg white, for brushing

Start by making the cookies. Heat the honey in a pan over medium heat, then add the sugar and spices, stirring all the while for about 5 to 7 minutes, until the sugar has dissolved (be careful the honey does not come to a boil). Remove from the heat and set aside to cool.

In a separate pan, only just melt the butter over medium heat, then set aside to cool.

Sieve the flour and the baking powder into a large bowl, pour in the cooled honey/spice mixture, the cooled melted butter, and the egg, and mix with a large wooden spoon to form a soft dough. Transfer into a smaller bowl and cover with plastic wrap. Refrigerate overnight.

The following day, mix all the ingredients for the filling in a bowl.

Preheat the oven to 350°F/180°C. Line a baking sheet with parchment paper.

Take the dough out of the refrigerator and divide it into halves. Return half to the refrigerator. Set the other half aside for 15 minutes before rolling it out. On a clean, floured work surface, roll out the dough to a thickness of ¼-inch using a floured rolling pin. Using a cookie cutter, cut into 2½-inch circles.

Place ½ teaspoon of the filling into the center of every other circle and cover with a plain circle, pressing down the edges to seal. Transfer the rounds to the lined baking sheet, setting each round ¾ inch apart. Brush the tops with egg white and place half an almond in the center of each cookie, pressing down gently. Bake for 20 minutes, to a deep golden-brown color. Remove from the oven, peel the cookies off the parchment paper, and cool on wire racks.

Incorporate any leftover dough into the remaining, refrigerated half of the dough and repeat the procedure until all the dough has been used.

Once the cookies have cooled completely, store in airtight containers. They will keep for several weeks in a cool, dark place.

Grazer Zwieback
GRAZ RUSKS

MAKES 22 SLICES

5 large egg white, room temperature

⅔ cup/3 oz confectioner's sugar

⅔ cup/2½ oz all-purpose flour, plus extra for dusting

Grated zest of ½ lemon

2 tbsp/1 oz unsalted butter, melted and cooled

Butter, for greasing

⅔ cup/3 oz confectioner's sugar mixed with 1 tsp homemade vanilla sugar (see page 136), for coating/dusting

Preheat the oven to 325°F/160°C.

In the bowl of an electric mixer, whisk the egg whites to soft peaks. Gradually add two-thirds of the confectioner's sugar, and whisk on a high speed until very stiff. Using a large metal spoon, fold in the remaining confectioner's sugar, along with the flour and grated lemon zest. Finally, carefully stir in the melted and cooled butter.

Grease and flour a 1-lb loaf pan. Transfer the mixture into the pan and bake for 45–50 minutes until golden brown. Remove from the oven and turn onto a wire rack to cool. Because it is such an airy cake, ideally it should be left to rest overnight. This helps it solidify and makes it easier to cut.

The following day, preheat oven to 300°F/150°C.

Using a serrated knife, thinly slice the loaf into ¼ inch slices. Coat both sides of each slice in the vanilla sugar and place on a baking sheet. Place in the oven for 20–25 minutes until golden brown, then turn over the slices and bake for a further 8–10 minutes. Remove from the oven and if you wish, dust lightly once more with vanilla sugar. Allow to cool completely before storing in airtight containers for up to three weeks. Not suitable for freezing.

Husarenkrapferln
THUMBPRINT COOKIES

MAKES 38

1¾ cups/7½ oz all-purpose flour, plus extra

⅓ cup/2½ oz superfine sugar

10 tbsp/5 oz cold unsalted butter, diced

2 large egg yolks

1 large egg white

1 oz blanched almonds, coarsely chopped

2½ tbsp/1 oz granulated sugar

¼ cup/3½ oz apricot or raspberry jam

Sift the flour into a food processor and add the superfine sugar and diced butter. Process until the mixture resembles coarse breadcrumbs. Turn out onto a clean work surface and make a well in the center. Add the egg yolks and mix together, using a metal spatula to draw in the flour. Press the dough into a ball, wrap it in plastic wrap, and refrigerate for 30 minutes to 1 hour, until firm.

Preheat oven to 325°F/160°C. Line a baking sheet with parchment paper.

Remove the dough from the refrigerator and form small 1-inch balls. Space them 1 inch apart on the baking sheet.

Tip a little flour into a small bowl. Dip the end of a wooden spoon into the flour and gently press the underside of the spoon into each ball, leaving a deep indentation in the center of each cookie.

Brush a little egg white over each cookie and sprinkle with the almonds and the granulated sugar. Some of the topping will inevitably end up on the baking sheet, but these sugary crumbs are delicious once cooked! Bake for 20–25 minutes, until golden brown. Remove from the oven and transfer the cookies to cooling racks.

In a saucepan over low heat, warm the jam to make it more spreadable and then let it cool. Once the cookies have cooled, spoon a little jam into the center of each. Allow the jam centers to cool completely (the jam will harden) before storing. Place a sheet of wax paper between each cookie for storage purposes. Store in airtight containers for up to one week or in the freezer for up to three months.

BLANCHING ALMONDS
If you are blanching your own almonds, drop the unpeeled almonds into a pan of boiling water. Cover and immediately remove from the heat. Allow to stand for 5 minutes, then drain and peel while still fairly hot. Pinch the end of each almond between your thumb and index finger — the skins will slide off effortlessly.

Honig-Butterkeks Mini

MINI'S HONEY BUTTER COOKIES

MAKES 32

FOR THE DOUGH

2¼ cup/10 oz all-purpose flour

¾ cup/3½ oz confectioner's sugar

14 tbsp/7 oz unsalted butter, at room temperature, plus extra for greasing

1 tsp homemade vanilla sugar (see page 136), or ½ tsp vanilla extract

Pinch of salt

1 egg white

FOR THE FILLING

Scant ⅓ cup runny honey

6 freshly shelled walnuts

3½ oz candied citrus peel

1 egg yolk

NOTE

Don't use fruits that have dried out and hardened. They will remain hard during baking.

Cream the butter in a stand mixer on medium speed until light, add the confectioner's sugar and continue beating until pale and fluffy. With a wooden spoon mix in vanilla sugar, salt and the flour, just until incorporated, and the dough begins to come away from the sides of the bowl.

Scrape the mixture onto two large sheets of plastic wrap. Use the wrap to press down on the dough with your knuckles just until it holds together. Wrap each piece loosely in plastic wrap and press down to form a flat disk. Refrigerate for approxiamely half an hour (watch carefully to make sure it doesn't become too hard).

Preheat oven to 350°F/180°C. Line two baking sheets with parchment paper. Remove the first batch of the chilled dough and place it in the center between two sheets of waxed paper. Using a rolling pin, roll out the dough to a thickness of ⅛ inch and cut out 2-inch rounds with a cookie cutter. Using an apple corer, stamp out the center of every other cookie.

Using a palette knife with a wide blade, carefully transfer the solid cookies to the baking sheet, brush each of the solid rounds with the egg white and place the holed round on top and return them to the refrigerator. Repeat the same procedure with the remainder of the dough. If the dough becomes too warm to handle, return it briefly to the refrigerator to chill again.

For the filling, combine the walnuts with the candied citrus peel in a food processor and process until very finely chopped. On low heat gently bring the honey to a boil, add the nut/fruit mixture, while stirring continuously and simmer for another minute. Set aside to cool.

Take out one of the baking sheets from the refrigerator, brush the rings with the egg yolk. Fill the center with a heaped ½ teaspoon of the filling. Bake for 16–20 minutes, rotating the sheet halfway through, or until cookies are tinged with gold all over and beginning to brown at the edges. (Keep a close eye on the timing.) Remove the baking sheet from the oven and let stand on a wire rack for 5 minutes. Transfer each cookie to wire racks to cool completely before storing them in airtight containers for up to one week, or up to two months in the freezer.

Ischler Törtchen

ISCHLER TARTLETS

MAKES 20

2 cups/9 oz all-purpose flour

10 tbsp/5 oz unsalted butter

⅓ cup/2½ oz superfine sugar

1½ oz ground almonds

1 large egg yolk

1 tbsp milk

⅓ cup/1½ oz confectioner's sugar

¼ cup/3½ oz apricot or red currant jam

Preheat the oven to 350°F/180°C.

Make sure all ingredients are cold. For this purpose, measure the flour into a metal bowl and refrigerate for 1 hour.

Sieve the flour into a food processor and add the diced butter. Process until the mixture resembles coarse breadcrumbs. Add the superfine sugar and ground almonds and mix again. Tip the mixture onto a clean work surface and make a well in the center. In a bowl, beat the egg yolk with the milk and then pour into the center of the flour mixture. Mix, first with a knife and then with your hands, until the dough holds together. Form the dough into a flat disc and divide it into two equal portions. Refrigerate half the dough.

Roll out the other half of the dough to a thickness of ⅛ inch and cut out 2½-inch rounds with a scalloped cookie cutter. Cut a hole in the center of every other cookie using an apple corer. Gather any scraps of dough and form them into a ball, then flatten into a disc. Wrap in plastic wrap and refrigerate until ready to use.

Gently transfer the cookies onto an ungreased baking sheet, leaving about an inch between each cookie. Bake for 12–15 minutes, until the edges start to color.

Remove from the oven and allow to cool on the baking sheet for about a minute, then transfer the cookies onto cooling racks to cool completely.

While the first batch of cookies is cooling, use up the remaining dough and the saved scraps in the same way.

Once the cookies have cooled, dust only those cookies with the hole in the center with confectioner's sugar. In a saucepan, warm the jam on low heat to make it more spreadable, then set aside to cool slightly. Sandwich the jam between the solid cookies and the dusted ones. Store in airtight containers for up to one week or in the freezer for up to three months.

Ischli Fank

SPICED COOKIES

MAKES 46

FOR THE COOKIES

20 tbsp/10 oz unsalted butter, at room temperature

Scant ⅔ cup/5 oz superfine sugar

1 large egg

½ tsp ground cinnamon

½ tsp ground cloves

1 scant tsp lemon zest

2¼ cups/10 oz all-purpose flour

5 oz ground almonds

½ cup set honey

FOR THE CHOCOLATE GLAZE

3½ oz (50% cocoa) chocolate, for glazing

Start by making the cookies. In the bowl of an electric mixer, cream the butter with the sugar until light and fluffy. Beat in the egg until it has been incorporated. Stir in the spices and the lemon zest.

Sift the flour into a large bowl and stir in the ground almonds, followed by the creamed butter, mixing all together. Cover with plastic wrap and refrigerate for 45 minutes. Remove the dough from the fridge and divide it into three equal portions. Roll each portion into a 2½-inch-wide sausage, then wrap each roll in waxed paper and refrigerate for 30–40 minutes.

Preheat the oven to 350°F/180°C.

Cut the rolls into ¼-inch-thick rounds. Place them on a baking sheet lined with parchment paper, leaving a little space between slices and bake for approximately 25 minutes until golden brown, then remove from oven. Once cooled, sandwich two cookies together with a little honey.

To make the chocolate glaze, break the chocolate into small pieces and place in a heatproof bowl. Melt the chocolate, either by heating in a microwave for 20–30 seconds or by placing in the center of an oven preheated to 200°F/100°C until it has melted to a silky smooth texture, about 10–15 minutes. Remove, stir until smooth and allow to cool slightly before spreading a thin layer over the top of each cookie.

Allow the cookies to cool. Store in airtight containers for up to one week or in the freezer for up to three months, placing a sheet of waxed paper between each layer of cookies.

Lebkuchen Gertraud Dergans

GINGERBREAD GERTRAUD

MAKES 40

¾ cup plus 1 tbsp dark, runny honey

Scant ⅔ cup/4½ oz granulated sugar

1 tsp ground cloves

3 tbsp ground cinnamon

1 tsp allspice

5½ tbsp/2½ oz unsalted butter

2 oz candied lemon peel

1 oz candied orange peel

1 oz almonds

4½ oz hazelnuts

3 large eggs

4 cups/17½ oz all-purpose flour

1 tsp baking soda dissolved in 1 tbsp water

Mix the honey and sugar in a pan. Place over medium heat and bring to a gentle boil, stirring regularly, until the sugar has dissolved. Remove from the heat and mix in the ground cloves, cinnamon and allspice. Set aside to cool.

In a separate pan, melt the butter and set aside to cool. Using a sharp knife, very finely chop the candied lemon and orange peel, almonds and hazelnuts (this can be done in a food processor if you prefer).

In a small bowl, beat two of the eggs until frothy. In a large bowl, sift the flour and add the melted butter mixture, the beaten eggs and the dissolved baking soda. Mix with a wooden spoon to incorporate all the ingredients. Use your hands to shape the mixture into a flat disc. Place the dough in a small bowl, cover with plastic wrap and refrigerate overnight.

The following day, preheat the oven to 325°F/160°C. Line a baking sheet with parchment paper.

Roll out the dough to a thickness of ¼ inch and cut out with a 2-inch round cookie cutter. Place the cookies on the prepared baking sheet and brush with the remaining egg, lightly beaten. Bake on the middle rack of the oven for 20–25 minutes until golden brown. Store in airtight containers for up to four weeks or in the freezer for up to three months.

Linzerli
LINZER COOKIES

MAKES 36

1⅔ cup/7 oz all-purpose flour, plus extra for dusting

1½ tsp cocoa powder

¾ tsp ground cinnamon

½ cup/4½ oz superfine sugar

9 tbsp/4½ oz unsalted butter, cold

1 large egg, lightly beaten

4½ oz ground almonds

Grated zest of ½ lemon

¼ cup/3½ oz raspberry jam (or runny honey)

1 large egg yolk, for brushing

Confectioner's sugar, for dusting

Preheat the oven to 350°F/180°C. Line a baking sheet with parchment paper.

Sift the flour into a food processor and add the cocoa powder, cinnamon, and sugar. Cut the butter into cubes and add to the flour. Process briefly until the mixture reseembles fine breadcrumbs. Add the ground almonds and lemon zest and process for a further 10 seconds.

Tip the mixture out onto a clean work surface and make a well in the center. Pour in the beaten egg and mix quickly, first with the tip of a knife and then with your hands. Work into a fairly firm dough, adding more flour if necessary.

Roll out the dough to a ¼-inch thickness. Cut the dough into rounds using a 2-inch round cookie cutter. Cut a hole in the center of every other cookie using an apple corer. Brush the whole rounds with either warmed and then cooled raspberry jam or honey. Use sparingly so that the jam doesn't bubble over during baking. Place a perforated cookie on top of each solid cookie. Lightly brush the tops of each cookie with egg yolk and place in the preheated oven. Bake for 25–30 minutes, watching in case they are ready a little earlier. If filled with raspberry jam dust with confectioner's sugar. If filled with honey, leave plain. Store in airtight containers for up to one week or in the freezer for up to three months.

Parmesan-Stangerln

PARMESAN STICKS

MAKES 28

1⅔ cup/7 oz all-purpose flour

10 tbsp/5 oz butter, cold

1 tsp salt

3 tbsp sour cream

1 egg yolk

Grated Parmesan cheese,
for sprinkling

Chill the flour in a bowl in the refrigerator for 30 minutes. Sieve the cold flour into a food processor and add the butter, diced. Process until the mixture resembles coarse breadcrumbs. Tip out onto a clean work surface, sprinkle over the salt, add the sour cream, and using the blade of a knife initially and then your hands, quickly bring the mixture into a ball. Divide the ball in two and shape each into a 2-inch-thick log. Place each on a plate, cover with plastic wrap, and refrigerate for 30 minutes.

Preheat the oven to 425°F/220°C. Line a baking sheet with parchment paper.

Take out one half of the dough from the refrigerator. Cut off small pieces of dough the size of a walnut and roll between your hands into 4 inch lengths. Place on the baking sheet and brush each with the egg yolk and sprinkle the grated Parmesan cheese liberally on top. Bake for 15 minutes to a rich golden color. Cheese can burn quickly, so do watch the sticks! Test one before removing the entire sheet. When done, transfer onto wire racks to cool. Repeat with the other half of the dough.

The sticks taste best while still warm and are delicious served for tea or with a salad.

Pfeffernüssli Elisabeth Gulacsy

ELISABETH GULACSY'S ALLSPICE COOKIES

MAKES 46

1 cup/9 oz superfine sugar

2 large eggs, at room temperature

¾ tsp ground nutmeg

½ tsp ground cinnamon

¼ tsp ground cloves

2½ oz candied citrus peel, very finely chopped

4½ oz ground almonds

2 cups/9 oz all-purpose flour, plus extra for dusting

Butter, for greasing

Mix all ingredients, except for the flour, in a large bowl or food processor. Gradually add the flour and knead or process to form a dough. (If you prefer slightly higher cookies, add a pinch of baking powder to the flour.) Roll out the dough on a clean, lightly floured work surface to a thickness of ½ inch. Cut out 2-inch rounds using a cookie cutter.

Lightly grease a baking sheet. Place the rounds on the baking sheet and set aside to rest overnight in a warm place.

The following day, preheat the oven to 300°F/150°C. Just before baking, turn the cookies over on the baking sheet and bake for approximately 30 minutes. Store in airtight containers for up to one week or in the freezer for up to three months.

Rumovè Kuličky
RUM BALLS

MAKES 68

8½ oz dark (70% cocoa) chocolate

10 oz ground walnuts

Scant 3 cups/12½ oz confectioner's sugar

8 tbsp dark rum

Granulated sugar, for coating

Break the chocolate into small pieces and place in a heatproof bowl. Melt the chocolate, either by heating in a microwave for 20–30 seconds or by placing the bowl over a pan of just simmering water. Make sure the bowl is not touching the water and monitor carefully. Alternatively you can melt the chocolate the way Hertha would have (see note below). Stir the chocolate until smooth and set aside to cool.

In a separate bowl, mix the ground walnuts, confectioner's sugar and rum together, and stir in the cooled chocolate. Gather into a large ball. Take a heaped teaspoon of the mixture and roll it between the palms of your hands to form 1-inch balls.

Pour the sugar into a shallow bowl and roll the rum balls in it until evenly coated. Place on a baking tray, cover with a sheet of wax paper and leave to set for several hours or overnight. Store in airtight container for up to two weeks. Not suitable for freezing.

NOTE

Put the chocolate pieces in an ovensafe bowl and place in the center of an oven preheated to 200°F/100°C until it has just melted to a silky smooth texture, about 10–15 minutes. Be sure to monitor the chocolate so that it does not burn. Remove from the oven, stir until smooth and set aside to cool.

Schokoladenkugeln

CHOCOLATE TRUFFLES

MAKES 20 TRUFFLES

7 oz dark (70% cocoa) chocolate

4 heaped tbsp of a mix of walnuts and coarsely chopped praline (see page 200) (optional)

3 tbsp/2 oz unsalted butter

Heaped ⅓ cup/ 2 oz confectioner's sugar

1 large egg, at room temperature

4 tbsp chocolate sprinkles (or 4 tbsp cocoa powder mixed with 1 tsp confectioner's sugar)

Break the chocolate into small pieces and place in a heatproof bowl. Melt the chocolate, either by heating in a microwave for 20–30 seconds or by placing the bowl over a pan of just simmering water. Make sure the bowl is not touching the water and monitor carefully. Alternatively you can melt the chocolate the way Hertha would have done (see note on page 122). Stir the chocolate until smooth and set aside to cool.

Pulse the nut mixture to a fine texture, but not so fine that it becomes a paste. Set aside.

In the (warmed) bowl of an electric mixer, cream the butter until it turns light in color. Beat in the confectioner's sugar, then the egg and continue to beat until all is incorporated. Add the cooled chocolate, beating all the while.

Using a wooden spoon, stir in the pulsed nuts. Refrigerate, uncovered, for a 1–1½ hours to firm up enough to make the rolling process possible.

Take a heaped teaspoon of the mixture and roll it between the palms of your hands to form 1-inch balls.

Pour the chocolate sprinkles and/or the cocoa powder into separate shallow bowls and roll the balls in the coating until evenly coated. Place on a baking tray, cover with a sheet of wax paper, and leave to set for several hours or overnight. Store in airtight containers for up to two weeks. Not suitable for freezing.

Schokoladentaferln mit Zitroneneis

CHOCOLATE WAFERS WITH LEMON GLAZE

MAKES 24

FOR THE COOKIES

1¼ cups/5½ oz all-purpose flour

7 tbsp/3½ oz unsalted butter, diced

½ cup plus 1 tbsp/2 oz superfine sugar

3 oz dark (65% cocoa) chocolate, grated

1 large egg yolk, or 2 small yolks

Scant 2 tbsp light cream or half and half, cold

FOR THE LEMON GLAZE

2 cups/9 oz confectioner's sugar

3–4 tbsp fresh lemon juice lemon

Mix the egg yolk with the cream and set aside. Preheat the oven to 350°F/180°C. Spray and line a baking sheet with parchment paper.

Chill the flour in a bowl in the freezer for at least 30 minutes before making the dough. Sift the flour into a food processor and add the butter. Process briefly until the mixture resembles course crumbs. Add the sugar and grated chocolate and process briefly to mix through. Tip the mixture out onto a clean working surface.

Make a well in the center of the flour mixture and pour in the yolk/cream while using the tip of a cold knife to initially help incorporate the liquid, then use your hands to quickly form the dough into a ball. Lightly flour the work surface, then roll out the dough evenly into a rectangle to a thickness of ¼-inch. With a sharp knife cut the dough into 2½- x 1½-inch rectangles.

Arrange the rectangles on the baking sheet and bake for 10–15 minutes, or until cookies just begin to brown around the edges. They burn easily, so watch closely.

Remove from the oven. Let cool on the baking sheet for 5 minutes before transferring them to wire racks to cool completely.

To make the glaze, sieve the confectioner's sugar into a bowl. Gradually add the strained lemon jouice, 1 teaspoon at a time, stirring continually to reach a moderately thick, spreadable consistency. Cover each thoroughly cooled wafer with a thin coat of glaze. Allow to dry completely (it does take a couple of hours), before storing them in airtight containers for a week or in the freezer for up to 2 months. They are at their prime within two days after baking!

Schokoladenkugeln Mini
MINI'S CHOCOLATE BALLS

MAKES 52

2 large eggs

Heaped ¾ cup/7 oz superfine sugar

9 oz whole unpeeled almonds, ground

4½ oz dark (70% cocoa) chocolate, grated

1 tsp ground cinnamon

2 tbsp all-purpose flour

Confectioner's sugar, for coating

Whisk the eggs with sugar until the mixture is a very pale color. Stir in the remaining ingredients (minus the confectioner's sugar). It is important that the mixing be done very quickly so that the mixture holds together.

Form 1-inch balls in the palms of your hands. Pour the confectioner's sugar into a shallow bowl and roll the balls in it until evenly coated.

Place on a well-greased baking tray to set for several hours, but not overnight.

When the balls have set, preheat the oven to 300°F/150°C. Bake for 25–30 minutes. As they bake, they expand and crack open – don't worry, this is all part of the process and does not compromise the delicious flavor! Store in airtight containers for up to one week or in the freezer for up to three months.

Schokoplätzchen

CHOCOLATE DROPS

MAKES 25

2 oz dark (70% cocoa) chocolate

5 tbsp/2½ oz unsalted butter

¾ cup/3½ oz confectioner's sugar

2½ oz ground almonds

Preheat the oven to 275°F/140°C.

Break the chocolate into small pieces and place in a heatproof bowl. Melt the chocolate, either by heating in a microwave for 20–30 seconds or by placing the bowl in a pan of just simmering water. Make sure the bowl is not touching the water and monitor carefully. Alternatively you can melt the chocolate the way Hertha would have done (see note on page 122). Stir the chocolate until smooth and set aside to cool.

Line a baking sheet with parchment paper. In the bowl of an electric mixer, beat the butter until light and fluffy. Stir in the confectioner's sugar and then the cooled chocolate. Finally stir in the ground almonds.

Drop a teaspoon of the mixture onto the prepared baking sheet (but do not flatten!). Space the drops about 2 inches apart as they will expand.

Bake for 55–60 minutes. As there is no real way of testing them to see if they are ready, keep a watch around the 50-minute mark to make sure they are not burning. Remove from the oven and transfer onto wire racks to cool. Store in airtight containers for up to two weeks or in the freezer for up to three months.

Spanischer Wind

MERINGUES

**MAKES 25 LARGE OR
50 SMALL MERINGUES**

**3 large egg whites,
at room temperature**

¾ cup/6 oz superfine sugar

Preheat the oven to 250°F/120°C. Line a baking sheet with parchment paper.

In the bowl of an electric mixer, beat the egg whites to stiff peaks. Gradually add one-third of the sugar, one tablespoon at a time, whisking all the while (this should take about 10 minutes). Carefully fold in the remaining sugar using a large metal spoon. The mixture will be stiff, silky-smooth, and glossy.

If you are making large meringues, drop a heaped tablespoon of the egg white onto the prepared baking sheet. If you prefer smaller meringues, use a heaped teaspoon. Meringues don't expand, so there is no need to space them too far apart. Bake on the bottom shelf of the oven for between 1½ and 2 hours (depending on size) until the meringues are firm with a hint of color. Turn the oven off but leave the meringues in the oven with the door closed to cool for another few hours or even overnight so that they dry out slowly. Store in airtight containers for several days. Not suitable for freezing.

NOTE

The small meringues were hung on the tree at Christmas time. You would place a short piece of cotton thread in a U-shape on the baking sheet and drop a teaspoon of egg white mixture at the open ends to seal them. When baked, you have built-in loops ready for hanging on the tree like beautiful drops of snow!

Weihnachtslebkuchen Tante Fränzchen

AUNT FRÄNZCHEN'S CHRISTMAS GINGERBREAD

MAKES 88

FOR THE GINGERBREAD

2 cups/9 oz confectioner's sugar

1 tsp baking soda

1 tsp ground cinnamon

1 tsp allspice

1 tsp ground cloves

4 cups/17½ oz all purpose flour, plus an extra ¾ cup if needed

1 cup runny honey

1 large egg, lightly beaten

FOR THE LEMON GLAZE

2 cups/9 oz confectioner's sugar

3–4 tablespoons of fresh lemon juice

Start by making the gingerbread. Line a baking sheet with parchment paper.

Sift all the dry ingredients onto a clean work surface (use only 4 cups of flour for now). Add the honey and the lightly beaten egg and knead into a pliable dough. If the dough feels a little wet and sticky, add a little more flour. Form the dough into a ball, patting it to flatten it a little, then cover with plastic wrap and refrigerate overnight.

The following day, preheat the oven to 325°F/160°C. Take one-third of the dough out of the fridge, leaving the rest wrapped, and roll it out to a thickness of ¼ inch. Cut out circles using a 2-inch cookie cutter. Place on the prepared baking sheet and bake for 25–30 minutes until medium brown in color; monitor them closely as they can burn very quickly. Remove from the oven and transfer to wire racks to cool. Repeat with the other two-thirds of the dough.

To make the lemon glaze, sieve the confectioner's sugar into a bowl. Gradually add the lemon juice, 1 teaspoon to start off with, then almost drop by drop, stirring between each addition to make sure the glaze doesn't get too runny. It should be of a spreadable consistency.

Store the gingerbread in airtight containers and glaze either immediately or up to three days after baking. They will take about four weeks to soften and be at their most flavorful. The cookies can be stored for up to six weeks, mellowing nicely with age.

NOTE

These gingerbread need to be made a minimum of four weeks in advance. They are rock hard when first baked but become soft and nicely chewy over time.

Glaze the gingerbread to your own imagination: give your artistic talent full reign during the season of advent! Use a teaspoon to decorate the surface of each gingerbread or glaze the entire surface.

Vanillekipferln

VANILLA SHORTBREAD CRESCENTS

MAKES 48

FOR THE SHORTBREAD

2¼ cups/10 oz all-purpose flour

Heaped ⅓ cup/2 oz confectioner's sugar, plus 1 tbsp vanilla sugar

15 tbsp/7½ oz unsalted butter, cold

3½ oz ground almonds

2 small egg yolks

FOR THE COATING

2 cups/9 oz confectioner's sugar

5 tbsp homemade vanilla sugar (see below)

3 tbsp/1½ oz superfine sugar

Preheat the oven to 350°F/180°C. Line a baking sheet with parchment paper.

Start by making the cookies. Sieve the flour into a food processor and add the confectioner's sugar. Dice the butter, add to the flour, and process until the mixture resembles coarse breadcrumbs. Add the ground almonds and the egg yolks and process again. Turn the mixture onto a clean, floured work surface and, using your hands, mix swiftly into a smooth dough.

Wrap the dough in plastic wrap and refrigerate for one hour. After this time, remove from the fridge, discard the plastic wrap, and break off small walnut-size pieces of dough. On a clean work surface, roll them into ½- x 2½-inch rolls. Bend into crecents and place onto the prepared baking sheet. Bake for 18–20 minutes, until golden.

In the meantime, prepare the coating. Sieve all three sugars into a large bowl and mix well.

When cooked, remove the crescents from the oven and immediately tip them into the coating, carefully rolling them in the sugar to coat them all over. This is an art indeed, as you have to work quickly while the crescents are still hot! You may have to work in batches, depending on the size of your bowl.

Once the crescents are all coated and still a little warm, place them into a cookie tin with a tight-fitting lid, placing a sheet of waxed paper between each layer. Let them cool in the tin with the lid on. Store for up to four weeks. Not suitable for freezing.

HOMEMADE VANILLA SUGAR

To make your own homemade vanilla sugar, run the blade of a sharp knife down the length of a vanilla pod to split it open. Cut these two lengths again. Do not scrape out the seeds! Place the split pods into a 1-cup glass jar filled with confectioner's sugar. The confectioner's sugar will take on the flavor of the vanilla within about a month and produce a lovely aromatic flavor. Vanilla sugar keeps for up to 6 months in a sealed jar and can be used as a replacement for the packaged variety, which has very little flavor.

Tiroler Klosterkipferln Tatjana

TATJANA'S TIROLIAN CONVENT CRESCENTS

MAKES 24

Heaped 1 cup/5 oz all-purpose flour

⅓ cup/1½ oz confectioner's sugar

7 tbsp/3½ oz cold unsalted butter, diced

3 oz ground roasted hazelnuts (see box)

1 tsp homemade vanilla sugar (see page 136), or ½ tsp vanilla extract

1½ oz dark (70% cocoa) chocolate, grated

1 tbsp candied citrus peel, crystalized ginger, very finely chopped

1 large egg yolk

3½ oz (50% cocoa) chocolate, melted

Sift the flour with the confectioner's sugar into a food processor and add the diced butter. Process until the mixture resembles coarse breadcrumbs. Add the ground hazelnuts, vanilla, grated chocolate, candied citrus peel, and egg yolk and process briefly again. Turn the mixture out onto a clean floured work surface and, using your hands, mix swiftly into a smooth dough.

Wrap the dough in plastic wrap and refrigerate for one hour. Preheat the oven to 350°F/180°C. Line a baking sheet with parchment paper.

After this time, remove from the fridge, discard the plastic wrap and break off small walnut-size pieces of dough. On a clean work surface, roll them into ½- x 2½-inch rolls. Bend into half-moons (crescents) and place onto the prepared baking sheet. Bake for 18–20 minutes, until golden, but not yet dark on the bottoms. Check after 18 minutes to be sure they don't burn. Remove from the oven and set aside to cool.

When cooled, dip both ends of the crescents into the melted chocolate and place on wax paper until the chocolate hardens. Store in airtight containers for up to four weeks. Not suitable for freezing.

ROASTING HAZELNUTS

Spread out the hazelnuts on a baking tray and place in a preheated 300°F/150°C oven. Toast for about 10 minutes until fragrant, watching that they don't burn (check one by removing the skin to see that there is a shade of color). Remove from the oven, place in a clean kitchen towel and rub the nuts together until the skins come off. Pulse the nuts briefly in a food processor.

Süße Mehlspeisen
SWEET DESSERTS

When I was a child visiting my Austrian grandmother, I was always excited when a *Süße Mehlspeise* was on the menu, a main course that although sweet, is often served as a light meal for lunch or an early dinner. An example would be a meal consisting of *Kaiserschmarren* (see page 148), a type of thick pancake mixed with raisins, chopped into small pieces and dusted with powdered sugar. Or a *Marillenknödel* (see page 146), a wonderfully aromatic and delicious sweet dumpling filled with the ripest of apricots (or plums) in season, rolled in buttered breadcrumbs and sprinkled with sugar. They are filled with the purest nostalgia of a warm late summer's day.

Perhaps the fruit justified the nutritional value of these dishes, but the memories of them, especially given my North American upbringing, always came with a slightly decadent feeling of eating something you really shouldn't be. Anyone who has grown up in Austria like my mother will also vividly recall these summer specialties.

Süße Mehlspeisen also incorporate sweetened breads and cakes, such as the famed *Gugelhupf* (see page 156), a plum tart or jam-filled doughnuts. These, however, remain strictly intended for tea or coffee breaks.

Apfelknödel

APPLE DUMPLINGS

SERVES 4

FOR THE DUMPLINGS

2¼ lb dessert apples, peeled, cored and finely cubed

1 tbsp granulated sugar

2 tbsp semolina

1 large egg

1¼-1½ cups/5-6 oz all-purpose flour

FOR THE COATING

8½ tbsp/4 oz unsalted butter

5 oz fine breadcrumbs

2½ tbsp/1 oz granulated sugar

Start by making the dumplings. Put the cubed apples in a bowl, stirring in the sugar and semolina and let stand for 1–2 hours, covered.

After this time, mix the egg into the apples. With a wooden spoon, stir in enough of the flour (starting with 1¼ cups, then adding up to ½ cup more) to reach the consistency of dough.

Bring a large pan of lightly salted water to a boil. With hands wet, scoop out a level tablespoon of the dough and roll it gently in the palms of your hands to form a ball, slightly smaller than the size of a golf ball. You will need to wet your hands regularly so that the dumplings don't stick to them.

Drop the dumplings into the boiling water, one at a time (you will need to cook them in batches as it is likely they won't all fit in the pan at the same time). The dumplings will sink to the bottom of the pan. Partially cover the pan and when the water has returned to a boil, lower the heat to a simmer. After 10–12 minutes, the dumplings will be ready and will have floated to the top. Simmer for another 2–3 minutes, then lift them out with a slotted spoon and into a colander to drain.

To make the coating, melt the butter in a large frying pan and fry the breadcrumbs until lightly browned. Add the drained dumplings and roll them in the crumb mixture for a couple of minutes so that they are evenly coated. Place this first batch of dumplings in a warmed 300°F/150°C oven while waiting for the second batch to cook.

Transfer the dumplings onto warmed plates, sprinkling liberally with the sugar and serve immediately. A stewed fresh fruit compote complements these dumplings perfectly.

Apfelschmarren Nora

NORA'S APPLE PANCAKE

MAKES 8 SLICES

2 large eggs

1½ cups whole milk

1 cup/4 oz all-purpose flour

1 tsp granulated sugar, depending on sweetness of fruit

Pinch of salt

4 tbsp/2 oz unsalted butter

1½ lb dessert apples (or 1 lb apples and ½ lb pears), peeled, cored and thinly sliced

Confectioner's sugar, for dusting

Preheat the oven to 400°F/200°C.

In the bowl of an electric mixer, beat the eggs until light. Then add the milk, flour, sugar, and salt, and beat on a lower speed to a thin batter.

Melt the butter in a 9 x 12-inch cast-iron roasting pan in the oven: it should be hot and bubbling but make sure it's not burning. Remove from the oven and spread the apples evenly in the pan, then return to the oven and bake for 20 minutes, until the apples are half cooked. Give them a good stir, then pour the batter over the top. Increase the oven temperature to 425°F/220°C and bake for another 15 minutes, until well-puffed and golden on top.

Place the pan onto a wire rack and cool for a few minutes. Dust with confectioner's sugar and cut into eight pieces before serving.

Béchamelstrudel

BÉCHAMEL STRUDEL

MAKES 8 SLICES

9 oz ready-made filo pastry

3½ tbsp/1¼ oz butter, melted, for brushing

FOR THE BÉCHAMEL

3 tbsp/2 oz butter

3 tbsp all-purpose flour

Generous ¾ cup whipping cream

4 large eggs, separated

1 tbsp sour cream

⅓ cup/2½ oz superfine sugar

2 oz raisins

FOR THE VANILLA SAUCE

2 large egg yolks

2 cups milk

4 tbsp/2 oz granulated sugar

½ vanilla pod

Start by making the béchamel. Melt the butter in a heavy-base saucepan, then whisk in the flour and cook for about a minute, until bubbling. Remove from the heat and add the whipping cream while stirring rapidly with a wooden spoon. Return to the heat, bring to a boil while stirring vigorously, then reduce to a simmer and cook for another 2 minutes.

Transfer the béchamel to a large bowl. When cooled, add the egg yolks one at a time, beating well after each addition. Stir in the sour cream and sugar.

Preheat the oven to 350°F/180°C. Position the rack in the upper third of the oven. Line a baking sheet with parchment paper.

In a separate bowl, beat the egg whites to stiff peaks. Unwrap the filo pastry sheets and lay them out onto a clean work surface. Working quickly, brush the first sheet with melted butter and position another sheet immediately on top, overlapping the first sheet slightly. Repeat with another sheet of filo pastry, until you have a rectangle about 10 x 7 inches. Gently fold the egg whites into the béchamel using a spatula and spread down the center of the pastry sheet. Sprinkle the raisins over the filling and brush the edges of the pastry sheet with melted butter. Roll up into a strudel shape.

Transfer carefully onto the prepared tray, shape into a crescent and brush the top and sides with the remaining butter. Bake for 45–55 minutes, until crisp and light brown but check the color after 35 minutes. Best served warm and with a vanilla sauce.

To make the vanilla sauce, whisk all the ingredients together in a medium-size heat-resistant bowl. Set over a pan of simmering water, being careful that the bowl does not touch the water. Whisk for at least 5 minutes, until thick and pale (the mixture should double in volume). Remove the vanilla pod.

Marillenknödel (oder Zwetschkenknödel)

APRICOT (OR PLUM) DUMPLINGS

MAKES 12

FOR THE DUMPLINGS

2 lb floury potatoes

2 cups/9 oz all-purpose flour, plus extra for dusting (or 1⅔ cups flour and ⅓ cup semolina)

3 tbsp/1½ oz unsalted butter, diced

1 tsp salt

1 large egg

2 lb very small ripe apricots or Italian plums

FOR THE COATING

8½ tbsp/4 oz unsalted butter

5 oz plain breadcrumbs

FOR DUSTING

2½ tbsp/1 oz superfine sugar (if using apricots)

2½ tbsp/1 oz superfine sugar mixed with 1 tsp ground cinnamon (if using plums)

Start by making the dumplings. Boil the potatoes in their skins and when cool enough to handle, peel them and cut them in half. Flour a clean work surface and mash the potatoes in a potato ricer directly onto the floured surface.

Sieve the flour and semolina, if using, onto a floured surface. Add the diced butter and use your fingertips to combine them, pinching until the mixture resembles coarse crumbs. Add the salt and the cooled, mashed potatoes and lightly mix. Make a well in the center of the mixture and add the egg. Knead the dough with your hands to form a soft dough, making sure not to overwork it. Cut the dough into two as it will be easier to handle when rolling.

Shape the dough into a roll about 2 inches in diameter. Cut it into 12 equal rounds, flatten each piece between your hands and place one apricot in each center. Wrap the dough around the fruit to completely encase it. Make sure there are no exposed parts of the fruit. Gently roll it into a smooth ball in the palm of your hand.

Bring a large pan of very lightly salted water to a boil. Drop the dumplings into the boiling water, one at a time (you will need to cook them in batches as it is likely they won't all fit in the pan at the same time). The dumplings will sink to the bottom of the pan. Partially cover the pan and when the water has returned to a boil, lower the heat to a simmer. After 10–15 minutes, the dumplings will be ready and will have floated to the top. Lift them out with a slotted spoon and into a colander to drain.

To make the coating, melt the butter in a frying pan and fry the breadcrumbs until lightly browned. Add the dumplings and roll them in the crumb mixture for a couple of minutes so that they are evenly coated. Place this first batch of dumplings in a warmed oven while waiting for the second batch to cook.

Transfer the dumplings onto warmed plates, sprinkling liberally with the sugar and serve immediately.

Kaiserschmarren
EMPEROR'S MESS

SERVES 2

1 cup/4½ oz all-purpose flour

Pinch of salt

1 cup milk

2 oz raisins, soaked in ⅓ cup rum for 5 minutes, then drained (optional)

4 large eggs, separated

3½ tbsp/1¾ oz butter

¼ cup/1 oz confectioner's sugar plus more for dusting

In a large bowl, mix the flour and salt, add the milk and whisk until smooth. Add 1 egg yolk at a time, whisking well between additions. Add the raisins, if using.

In a separate bowl, beat the egg whites until very stiff. Fold them gently into the batter using a balloon whisk until well incorporated.

Heat a cast-iron frying pan over medium to high heat. Melt a heaped tablespoon of the butter until it bubbles. Quickly add about one-third of the batter to cover the bottom of the pan, distributing it evenly and immediately reducing the heat to low. Cover with a lid for 2½ minutes, then check to see if the bottom is golden. If it is, turn the pancake over and add a little more of the butter into the pan. It doesn't matter if the pancake breaks up while you're flipping it. Cover with the lid once more and after 1–2 minutes, check if the underside is golden. Sieve one-third of the confectioner's sugar over the pancake.

Using two tablespoons, roughly tear the dough into 1 to 2-inch pieces, and stir the pieces for a few minutes in the pan so that they become golden on all sides. Transfer to a serving plate to keep warm. Repeat twice more with the remaining two-thirds of the batter, or until all of the batter has been used. Serve while hot and crisp on warmed plates and dust with confectioner's sugar. *Kaiserschmarren* is traditionally served with stewed plums, or any other stewed fruit.

Kaiserschmarren is a beloved Austrian dish served as a dessert or main dish. *Kaiser*, meaning Emperor in German, and *Schmarrn*, Austrian slang for a kind of mishmash or poppycock, provides us with the charming literal translation of "the Emperor's mess," referring to Emperor Franz Josef I, who ruled Austria from 1848 to 1916. Speculation as to the origins of the dish are varied, but a popular favorite is that it was inadvertently created by the Emperor's cook. Whenever the Emperor's pancakes did not turn out perfectly because they were too thick or because they tore in the cooking process, they were served to his servants as *Kaiserschmarren*.

Palatschinken
SWEET CRÊPES

MAKES 12

FOR THE CRÊPES

1¼ cup/5 oz all-purpose flour

1 cup whole milk
(or ½ cup milk and
½ cup light cream)

2 large eggs

2 large egg yolks

¼ tsp salt

1 tsp superfine sugar

3½ tbsp/2 oz unsalted butter

CURD CHEESE FILLING

3½ tbsp/2 oz unsalted butter

Heaped ⅓ cup/2 oz
confectioner's sugar

2 large eggs

9 oz curd cheese, sieved
through a fine mesh

½ cup sour cream

Grated zest of 1 lemon

2 oz raisins

A little milk

Vanilla sugar (see page 136),
to taste

Jam of your choice (we favor
apricot or raspberry)

Start by making the crêpes. In a large bowl, mix all the ingredients to a batter. Melt a knob of butter in a frying pan over medium-high heat. Pour a small ladleful of batter into the pan. Tilt the pan quickly so that the batter thinly covers the surface of the pan. Fry over medium heat until golden on one side. Turn over and fry the other side.

Stack the crêpes one on top of each other on a plate and keep warm in a low oven until all crêpes have been cooked.

Spread a thin layer of jam onto each crêpe. Roll them up and serve dusted with vanilla sugar. Alternatively, you can fill them with a curd cheese filling. To make the filling start by preheating the oven to 350°F/180°C.

Cream the butter until light using an electric mixer. Add the confectioner's sugar and cream until light and fluffy. Add one egg at a time, beating well between each addition. With a wooden spoon, mix in the sieved curd cheese, sour cream, lemon zest, raisins, and finally, as much milk as is needed to make a spreadable mixture that is the consistency of jam.

Spread each crêpe with the filling. Fold in quarters and place them in a buttered ovensafe dish and bake for 10–15 minutes.

Buchteln

SWEET JAM BUNS

MAKES 16

¾ oz compressed yeast

¼ cup/2 oz superfine sugar

Scant ¾ cup milk

2¾ cups/12 oz bread flour

Pinch of salt

2 large egg yolks

4 tbsp unsalted butter, melted and cooled

Grated zest of ½ lemon and ½ orange

2½–3½ oz jam, such as apricot or plum (see page 219)

3 tbsp/1½ oz unsalted butter, melted

Confectioner's sugar, for dusting

Make sure all the kitchen equipment and ingredients are at room temperature.

Cream the yeast with 1 teaspoon of the sugar and gradually add the milk. Set in a warm place to proof: a preheated 212°F/100°C oven that has been turned off works well for this purpose.

Sift the flour with the salt into a warmed bowl.

In a separate bowl, whisk the egg yolks and the remaining sugar, and stir this into the flour with the yeast mixture, just as it starts to bubble and has risen to double its size. Mix in the butter and lemon and orange zest and beat with a wooden spoon, until the dough begins to "blister" (i.e. it has a satiny sheen and pulls away from the bowl). Turn the dough out onto a floured work surface and knead it until it feels smooth and elastic, for about 7–10 minutes. Add a little flour if the dough sticks to the surface. Shape into a ball and transfer it into an oiled bowl, rolling the ball around to coat it lightly in the oil. Cover with a clean dish towel.

Set the dough in a warm place, away from any drafts, ideally near a sun-lit spot. Leave to rise for 1–1¼ hours, until doubled in size: the length of time this takes depends on the room temperature and the temperature of the ingredients and tools being used.

When the dough has doubled in size, transfer it to a floured work surface. Knead it for a few seconds and roll it into a ½-inch-thick rectangle. Cut into 16 2½-inch squares. Put 1 teaspoon of jam in the center of each square. Gather the four corners and pinch them together to encase its contents.

Dip each packet into the melted butter, keeping some of the butter in reserve, and then place, sealed-sides down, onto a warmed, well-buttered 11-inch round cast-iron dish. The buns should crowd and touch each other in the pan. Cover with a dish towel and leave to rise in a warm place once more for about 45–60 minutes. Preheat the oven to 375°F/190°C.

Just prior to baking, brush the tops of the buns with the remaining melted butter and bake in the oven for 25–30 minutes until the buns pull away from the sides of the baking dish, and are golden brown on top. Immediately turn them over onto a wire rack to cool, then dust with confectioner's sugar and separate them to serve.

Gebackene Mäuse

DEEP-FRIED "MICE"

MAKES 21

¾ oz compressed yeast

3 tbsp/1½ oz granulated sugar

Generous ¾ cup tepid whole milk

2¾ cups/12 oz all-purpose flour

½ tsp salt

1 large egg

3½ tbsp/2 oz unsalted butter, melted and cooled

Grated zest of 1 lemon

2 oz raisins, soaked in 1–2 tbsp light rum for 30 minutes

Sunflower (or canola) oil, for deep-frying

Confectioner's sugar, for dusting

Make sure all the kitchen equipment and ingredients are at room temperature.

Cream the yeast with 1 teaspoon of the sugar and gradually add the milk. Set in a warm place to proof: a preheated 212°F/100°C oven that has been turned off works well for this purpose.

Sift the flour with the salt into a warmed bowl.

In a separate bowl, whisk the egg and the remaining sugar, and stir this into the flour with the yeast mixture, just as it starts to bubble and has risen to double its size. Mix in the butter and lemon zest and beat with a wooden spoon, until the dough has a satiny sheen and pulls away from the bowl. Turn the dough out onto a floured work surface and knead it until it feels smooth and elastic, for about 7–10 minutes. Add a little flour if the dough sticks to the surface. Mix in the drained raisins. Shape into a ball and transfer to an oiled bowl, rolling the ball around to coat it lightly in the oil. Cover with a clean dish towel. A more welcoming, less labor-intensive option, should it be available, is to use an electric mixer with a dough hook.

Set the dough in a warm place, away from any drafts, ideally near a sun-lit spot. Leave to rise for 1–1½ hours, until doubled in size: the length of time this takes depends on the room temperature and the temperature of the ingredients and tools being used.

Heat the oil in a deep-fryer to a temperature of 315°F–325°F (157°C–163°C). When the dough has doubled in size, punch it down once with your fist to deflate. Dip a tablespoon into the hot oil and scoop out a portion of dough. Slide the dough from the oily spoon onto a dry tablespoon and then let the dough glide into the hot oil. It will slide off the spoon easily. Continue in this manner with as many spoonfuls as will fit in the pan without overcrowding. When the dough hits the oil and loses some of its shape, little creatures resembling mice with small curly tails will form.

Turn the "mice" over with tongs once the underside has turned a deep golden color and wait for the other side to color. Don't rush this step! Test one by breaking it in half to see if the inside is fully baked with no trace of raw dough. Lift out the golden mice with a slotted spoon or tongs, drain on paper towels set over a wire rack. Dust with confectioner's sugar when the mice have cooled slightly. They are best served warm.

Mohnbeugel
POPPYSEED CRESCENTS

MAKES 18

FOR THE FILLING

½ cup whole milk

⅓ cup/2½ oz superfine sugar

4 oz ground poppyseeds

Grated zest of 1 small lemon

¾ oz raisins soaked in
2 tsp rum for 30 minutes

Pinch of ground cinnamon

FOR THE DOUGH

½ oz compressed yeast

¼ cup whole milk, cold

1¾ cups/8 oz bread flour

Pinch of salt

8½ tbsp/4 oz unsalted butter,
at room temperature

1½ tbsp/¾ oz superfine sugar

1 large egg yolk

1 large egg, for brushing

Start by making the filling. In a saucepan, bring the milk and sugar to a gentle boil. Stir in the poppy seeds, then reduce the heat to a simmer and stir regularly for 15 minutes. Remove from the heat and stir in the lemon zest, rum-soaked raisins and the cinnamon. Set aside to cool.

To prepare the dough, dissolve the yeast in the milk. Sieve the flour onto a clean work surface and add the salt. Cut in the butter with a knife and crumble with your fingertips until the mixture resembles coarse crumbs. Mix in the sugar and make a well in the center. Add the egg yolk with the dissolved yeast mixture and stir with the knife and then begin to gather all the ingredients into a ball with your hands, kneading it into a smooth dough. Leave the dough to rest on the work surface for 45 minutes covered with a clean dish towel.

After the resting period, knead the dough briefly and form it into a 10-inch-long log. Cut it in half lengthwise and divide each half into nine equal rounds with a sharp knife. Place each round onto a lightly floured work surface. Using only the ball of your hand, spread the shape into an oval the size of a good-sized palm. Place a small teaspoon of the filling in the center of the dough, then fold over the dough and press the edges together. Shape into crescents and place each piece 3 inches apart onto a baking sheet lined with parchment paper, making sure the seams are face down. Brush the surface of each crescent with beaten egg, then leave them to rise in a warm place for 45 minutes.

Preheat the oven to 350°F/180°C. Bake the crescents for 18–20 minutes until golden brown. Remove from the oven and transfer onto wire racks to cool.

Gugelhupf mit Germ
YEAST-BASED GUGELHUPF

SERVES 6

2 oz flaked almonds

¾ oz compressed yeast

⅓ cup/2½ oz superfine sugar

1 cup tepid milk

4 cups/16 oz all-purpose flour, sifted

17 tbsp/9oz unsalted butter, at room temperature

3 large egg yolks

1 large egg

Grated zest of 1–2 lemons, to taste

Pinch of salt

2½ oz raisins, floured

Vanilla sugar (see page 136) or confectioner's sugar, for dusting

Make sure all the ingredients and kitchen equipment are at room temperature. The yeast can be set on top of the stove to warm.

Grease and lightly flour a ring mold. Sprinkle with the flaked almonds, which should stick to the sides.

Cream the yeast with a teaspoon of the sugar and about three-quarters of the tepid milk and one teaspoon of the flour. Mix and set aside in a warm place to rise for 15–20 minutes.

In the bowl of an electric mixer, cream the butter, gradually adding in the sugar. Add one egg yolk at time, beating well between each addition. Then beat in the whole egg. Stir in the grated lemon zest, salt, and a little of the flour, then the yeast mixture and the remaining flour and milk. Beat well with a wooden spoon until the dough comes off the sides of the bowl. If done by hand, this should take about 5 minutes. Add the raisins. Pour the dough into the mold. Cover with a dry, clean dish towel and place in warm spot to rise until the dough comes to within an inch of the top of the mold. This should take 50–60 minutes.

Preheat the oven to 350°F/180°C. Bake for 50–60 minutes, but reduce the heat to 250°F/120°C for the last 20 minutes.

Remove from the oven allow to cool in the mold before turning it over onto a flat surface. Once completely cooled, dust liberally with vanilla sugar or confectioner's sugar.

Traditionally, there's an option to make a *Gugelhupf* either with yeast or with baking powder. Though yeast sounds a little more complicated, the flavor is much more satisfying. In Hertha's bygone era cooks would sit with bowls between their laps and work the dough for what seemed like hours. Today, a packet of yeast and a food processor make life much easier, and the taste identical.

Kärtner Reindling
CARINTHIAN RING CAKE

SERVES 6

FOR THE DOUGH

¾ oz compressed yeast

Scant ¼ cup/2 oz superfine sugar

Scant ¾ cup milk

2¾ cups/12 oz bread flour

Pinch of salt

1 large egg yolk

5 tbsp/2½ oz unsalted butter, melted and cooled

Grated zest of 1 lemon

FOR THE FILLING

2 oz figs or prunes, chopped

2 oz walnuts, chopped

2 oz raisins

1 oz candied orange or mixed citrus peel

1½ tbsp/¾ oz dark brown soft sugar

1 tsp ground cinnamon

1½ tbsp/¾ oz unsalted butter, melted

FOR THE GLAZE (OPTIONAL)

1 cup/3½ oz confectioner's sugar

3–4 tbsp rum

Make sure all the ingredients and kitchen equipment are at room temperature.

Generously grease and flour a deep, 10-inch round cast-iron casserole dish.

Start by making the dough. Cream the yeast with one teaspoon of the sugar and the milk. Set in a warm place to proof for 8–10 minutes. The yeast can be set on top of the oven to warm.

Sift the flour with the salt into a warmed bowl. In a separate bowl, whisk the egg yolk and the remaining sugar, and stir this into the flour with the yeast mixture, just as it begins to bubble and has risen to double its size. Mix in the butter and lemon zest and beat with a wooden spoon, until the dough begins to "blister" (i.e., it has a satiny sheen and pulls away from the bowl). Turn the dough out onto a floured work surface and knead it until it feels smooth and elastic, for about 7–10 minutes. Add a little flour if the dough sticks to the surface. Shape into a ball and transfer it into an oiled bowl, rolling the ball around to coat it lightly in the oil. Cover with a clean dish towel. A more welcoming, less labor-intensive option, should it be available, is to use an electric mixer with a dough hook.

Set the dough in a warm place, away from any drafts, ideally near a sun-lit spot. Leave to rise for 45–60 minutes, or until doubled in size: the length of time this takes depends on the room temperature of the ingredients and tools being used.

In the meantime, mix all the ingredients for the filling together, minus the melted butter, and set aside.

Once the dough has doubled in size, roll it out on to a floured work surface to a ¼-inch-thick rectangle 9 x 16 inches in size. Sprinkle the filling over the dough, leaving a ¼-inch border all round, then dribble the melted butter over the filling. Using a rolling pin, gently press the filling into the dough. Roll up the dough lengthwise into a cylinder, pressing the seam to seal it.

Shape the roll into a circle, overlapping and sealing the ends firmly. Transfer the ring, seam-side down into the casserole dish. Cover with a dish towel and leave in a warm place to rise again for another 40–45 minutes, or until well risen.

Preheat the oven to 350°F/180°C. Bake for approximately 1 hour, until medium brown. If the top is browning too quickly, cover the casserole with parchment paper. Remove from oven and allow to cool a little in the dish, then turn the ring onto a wire rack and while still warm, dust with confectioner's sugar. If desired, you can pour a rum glaze zigzagged over the ring. To make the glaze, sift the confectioner's sugar into a bowl and stir in the rum, 1 teaspoon at a time, until smooth and of a glaze-like consistency.

Zwetschkengermfleck

PLUM CAKE

SERVES 6

¾ oz compressed yeast

⅓ cup/2½ oz granulated sugar

Scant ¾ cup tepid whole milk

2¾ cup/12 oz bread flour

Pinch of salt

1 large egg yolk

Grated zest of 1 lemon

4 tbsp/2 oz unsalted butter, softened

10½ oz small plums, washed, quartered, and pits removed

Egg white, for brushing

Confectioner's sugar, for dusting (optional)

In a warm bowl, mix the yeast with one teaspoon of the sugar. Add a little of the tepid milk to form a paste. Add the rest of the milk with one teaspoon of the flour. Set aside to rise in a warm place for about 8–10 minutes.

In a large warmed bowl, sift the remaining flour, salt, the remaining sugar, egg yolk, lemon zest, and the risen yeast. Lastly, add the softened butter. Using a wooden spoon, beat until the dough becomes shiny and pulls away from the wooden spoon and the sides of the bowl. Cover the bowl with a clean dish towel and leave it to rise in a warm place until almost doubled in size. This should take about 50 minutes.

Grease and lightly flour a 10- x 14-inch baking tray that is about an inch deep. When the dough has risen, knead it briefly on a floured surface. Take two-thirds of the dough, and with the palms of your wet hands, stretch it carefully out over the surface of the pan. The dough should be quite thin. Place the plums on the dough in rows so that they are touching each other and cover the surface of the dough. Sprinkle with sugar.

If desired, prepare a lattice with the remaining third of the dough. This is optional as it is time-consuming, but very traditional and makes the cake look very pretty. Roll out the dough and make thin rolls about the thickness of a finger and place over the plums in a lattice pattern. Brush the tops of lattice with egg white. Let it rise once more for 30 minutes. Preheat the oven to 375°F/190°C.

Bake for about 35–40 minutes, until the top is golden brown and the plums are thoroughly cooked. For an extra-sweet touch, dust with confectioner's sugar while the cake is still warm.

Streuselkuchen

CRUMBLE CAKE

SERVES 6

FOR THE DOUGH

⅓ oz fresh compressed yeast

2 tsp/⅓ oz granulated sugar

¼ cup tepid whole milk

Heaped 1 cup/5 oz bread flour

Pinch of salt

2 egg yolks

2 tbsp/1 oz unsalted butter, melted and cooled

Grated zest of 1 medium lemon

FOR THE TOPPING

¾ cup/3½ oz all-purpose flour

1½ oz ground almonds

¼ cup/2 oz soft dark brown sugar

1 tsp ground cinnamon

Grated zest of 1 small lemon

4 tbsp/2 oz unsalted butter, melted

Grease and flour a 3-inch deep, 10-inch square cast-iron baking dish.

Start by making the dough. Cream the yeast with one teaspoon of the sugar and milk. Set aside to prove for 8–10 minutes.

Sift the flour with the salt into a warm bowl. Make a well in the center and add the egg yolks, remaining sugar, cooled melted butter, lemon zest, and the proofed yeast. Mix and beat with a wooden spoon for about 10–15 minutes, until the dough becomes smooth and shiny. Using the dough hook on an electric mixer will simplify this arduous procedure.

Shape the dough into a ball and cover the bowl with a clean dish towel. Leave it in a warm place to rise to double its size. Depending on the room temperature, this will take about 1 hour.

In the meantime, make the topping. Mix all the ingredients together (except for the butter). Then pour the melted butter into the dry mixture and stir gently: the topping should be in the form of clumps.

Once the dough has risen, punch it down with your fist to deflate and knead it briefly on a floured surface. Place it into the prepared baking dish, using your knuckles to press it into all four corners. Sprinkle the topping evenly to cover the dough. Cover with a clean dish towel and set aside to rise once more for 45–60 minutes, until doubled in size.

Preheat the oven to 375°F/190°C. Bake for 35–45 minutes, then remove from the oven and carefully remove the cake from the dish.

Kuchen und Schnitten

CAKES AND GÂTEAUX

For me, cakes and gâteaux seemed initially daunting to attempt, but for my Austrian mother, they come as naturally as breathing and are made with the precision and delicacy of a surgeon. High-quality ingredients such as fresh hazelnuts and almonds, cinnamon, raisins, cloves, and seasonal fruits like cherries, apples, and plums provide pure, refined and rich yet delicate tastes. Once you learn that egg whites are only whipped on their own or with a little bit of sugar and only ever gently folded into a batter, that butter is creamed, with the magic words *until light and fluffy*, that chocolate must always be dark and of the highest quality, and that a springform pan is as essential as fresh farm eggs and unsalted butter, then you are, well, almost half-way there.

Apfelschlangel Elsa
ELSA'S APPLE SLICES

SERVES 6–8

FOR THE DOUGH

1½ cups/6½ oz all-purpose flour

1 tsp baking powder

5½ tbsp/2¼ oz cold, unsalted butter, diced, plus extra

¼ cup/3½ oz superfine sugar

1 large egg

FOR THE FILLING

1⅔ lb cooking apples, peeled, cored, and finely sliced

Scant ½ cup/3½ oz granulated sugar

2 oz raisins

Grated zest of one lemon

1 egg white

Confectioner's sugar

Preheat the oven to 350°F/180°C. Line a 10- x 15-inch baking sheet with parchment paper.

Start by making the dough. All ingredients for the dough should be cold. Sieve the flour along with the baking powder into a food processor and then add the diced butter.. Process until the mixture resembles coarse breadcrumbs. Mix in the sugar, then add the egg to form a dough that can be easily rolled out. Shape the dough into a ball, wrap it in plastic wrap, and refrigerate for at least 30 minutes.

To make the filling, heat a frying pan on medium to low heat and "fry" the apples (without any oil or butter) until most of the moisture has evaporated. Set aside to cool. Just before spreading the filling, stir in the sugar, raisins, and lemon zest.

Remove the dough from the fridge and roll it out so that it is slightly longer than the baking sheet and about ¼-inch thick. Carefully transfer the dough onto the lined baking sheet so that it is slightly overhanging.

Spread the cold apple filling along the center, lengthwise. Fold over the short ends by 1 inch on each side, then lift one long end up and over the filling, brush it with egg white, and fold the other long end over so it overlaps the center. Press down gently along the seam. Make sure all is well sealed and tucked in so that none of the mixture can escape. Bake for 40–45 minutes until golden.

Dust generously with confectioner's sugar once cooled. Cut into slices and serve with a dollop of whipped cream (optional).

Apfelstrudel
APPLE STRUDEL

MAKES 12 SLICES

FOR THE PASTRY

2 cups/9oz all-purpose flour, plus extra for dusting

1 heaped tsp butter, at room temperature

½ cup warm water

Pinch of salt

1 tsp white wine vinegar

1 large egg

3½ tbsp/2 oz butter, melted, for brushing

FOR THE FILLING

3½ oz plain breadcrumbs, pan-fried in a little butter and cooled

2¼ lb cooking apples, peeled, cored and very thinly sliced

Scant ½ cup/3½ oz granulated sugar

Pinch of ground cinnamon

2 oz raisins

7 tbsp/3½ oz unsalted butter, melted

Confectioner's sugar, for dusting

Sift the flour on to a work surface and make a well in the center. Place the butter into the warm water and pour it into the well along with the salt, vinegar, and the egg. Work it in using the tip of a knife, then use your hands to incorporate all the flour. If the mixture is too dry, add a little more warm water. Form into a ball.

Flour the work surface and knead the pastry for 5–7 minutes, by picking it up and throwing it down until it is shiny and smooth. Gather into a ball and cover with a large upturned bowl. Leave to rest for at least 30 minutes–1 hour. Preheat the oven to 350°F/180°C. Line a baking sheet with parchment paper.

Cover a table with a cotton sheet and lightly sprinkle it with flour. Place the pastry in the center and roll it out as far as it will go into a circle. Sparingly brush the melted butter around the edges of the rolled-out pastry. Carefully slide your hands between the pastry and the sheet. Starting at the center and working outwards, stretch the pastry out with the backs of your hands. Don't worry about any small tears. Continue to work outwards into all directions, as the pastry becomes almost paper-thin.

Cover two-thirds of the pastry (leaving one-third at the top uncovered), first with the breadcrumbs, then with the apples, sugar, cinnamon, and raisins. Brush the uncovered third with the melted butter, reserving some for glazing the top. Cut away any rough edges. Roll it up with the help of the sheet, starting at the filled end, as you would with a Swiss roll.

Carefully transfer the roll to the baking sheet, shaping it like a horseshoe. Brush the top with the remaining melted butter and bake for 40–45 minutes until golden and crisp. Serve warm, sprinkled generously with confectioner's sugar.

NOTE
Ready-made filo pastry makes a good, if not entirely authentic, alternative to making your own strudel dough.

Baiserschnitten
MERINGUE BARS

MAKES 8

FOR THE DOUGH

Heaped 1⅓ cups/6 oz all-purpose flour

½ tsp baking powder

Pinch of salt

2 tbsp confectioner's sugar

1 tsp ground cinnamon

7 tbsp/3½ oz unsalted butter, cold

Grated zest of ½ lemon

2 large egg yolks

Scant 2 tbsp ice-cold water

FOR THE MERINGUE

2 oz raisins

2 oz currants

2 oz blanched almonds

Grated zest of ½ lemon

2 large egg whites

Scant ½ cup/3½ oz superfine sugar

7 oz red currant jam for brushing over pastry

Chill the flour in a bowl for 30 minutes before making the dough. Then sieve the cold flour into a food processor with the baking powder, salt, confectioner's sugar and cinnamon. Dice the butter, add to the flour and process until the mixture resembles coarse breadcrumbs.

Add the lemon zest and process again. Tip the mixture out onto a clean work surface and create a small well in the center. Using the blade of a knife, mix in the egg yolks with 1 tablespoon of the ice-cold water to bring the dough together. Using your hands, knead swiftly, until incorporated. At this stage, it may be necessary to add part or all of the remaining water (the dough should be pliable but not too soft). Shape into a ball and flatten slightly. Place on a plate, cover with plastic wrap and refrigerate for 30 minutes.

Preheat the oven to 375°F/190°C. Line a 10- x 14-inch baking sheet with parchment paper.

In a small saucepan warm the jam, then set aside to cool.

Take the dough out of the fridge, remove the plastic wrap, and roll it out to the size of the baking sheet, minus an inch on each long side. Cut the dough lengthwise into three equal strips and transfer each strip onto the baking sheet, leaving a gap between each strip. Lightly prick the surface of the dough with a fork and bake for 20–25 minutes, until golden and only partially baked.

Meanwhile, make the meringue. Chop the raisins, currants, almonds, and lemon zest to a medium-fine consistency. Alternatively, you can whiz them very quickly in a food processor but be mindful not to over-process them into a paste.

In a medium bowl, whisk the egg whites to soft peaks using an electric mixer, then add the sugar, one tablespoon at a time, whisking all the while until two-thirds of the sugar has been incorporated and the whites start to look glossy. Fold in the remaining sugar using a large metal spoon. Fold the chopped fruits and almonds into the meringue using a spatula or metal spoon.

Remove the partially baked pastry from the oven and turn the temperature down to 275°F/140°C.

Brush a thin layer of the cooled red currant jelly over each pastry strip. Equally distribute the meringue mixture over the strips, using a spatula to even out the mixture. Return to the oven and bake for another 30 minutes, until the meringue is tinged with color and feels firm to the touch.

Remove from the oven, allow to cool, then cut into 2-inch slices using a sharp knife. Store in airtight containers for up to 3 days.

Blitzkuchen

LIGHTNING CAKE

MAKES 12 SLICES

FOR THE BASE

6 large egg yolks, room temperature

⅔ cup/5½ oz granulated sugar

½ cup plus 2 tbsp/3 oz all-purpose flour, sieved

4 large egg whites, room temperature

Juice of 1 lemon, strained

FOR THE TOPPING

½ cup/7 oz apricot jam

2 large egg whites, room temperature

1 cup/7 oz superfine sugar

¾ cup/2½ oz flaked almonds

Preheat the oven to 375°F/190°C for 20–30 minutes. Grease and line a 10- x 14- x 1-inch baking sheet with parchment paper.

Start by making the base. In the bowl of an electric mixer, whisk the egg yolks with the granulated sugar starting at medium and gradually increasing to medium-high speed for at least 5 minutes, until pale and fluffy and doubled in volume. Stop the mixer. Add the strained lemon juice, then lightly fold in the sieved flour with a metal spoon.

Thoroughly wash the beaters and in a separate bowl, whisk the egg whites until they form soft peaks and then fold into the batter, using the metal spoon until just incorporated. Spread the mixture evenly onto the prepared baking sheet and bake for about 10–15 minutes until light in color. Remove from oven and set aside to cool. Reduce the oven temperature to 300°F/150°C.

To make the topping, melt the jam in a saucepan on low heat, pour into a sieve, press through with a wooden spoon, and set aside to cool. Spread the cooled jam over the partially baked, and cooled base. In the bowl of an electric stand mixer, whisk the egg whites on medium speed until they become foamy. Gradually raise the speed to medium-high and beat until soft peaks form when the beater is raised. Add the confectioner's sugar, one tablespoon at a time, until all of it is used and the meringue becomes stiff and glossy. Now spread the meringue over the jam, covering it entirely. Sprinkle the flaked almonds over the top and return to the oven for approximately 10–15 minutes, or until the meringue has set and almonds are very lightly colored.

This recipe is symbolic as it is the first recipe entry in Tante Hertha's collection. *Blitz* means lightning, but it also connotes fast movement. The preparation may not be quite as "lightning fast" as some of today's modern recipes, but these sweet delights are well worth the effort.

Braune Apfelschnitten
BROWNED APPLE SLICES

MAKES 8–10 SLICES

FOR THE FILLING

1⅔ lb cooking apples, peeled, cored, and coarsely shredded

¼ cup/2 oz superfine sugar

FOR THE DOUGH

¼ cup/2 oz all-purpose flour

11 tbsp/6 oz unsalted butter, cold

4 tbsp superfine sugar

1 oz ground almonds

2 oz dark (70% cocoa) chocolate, finely grated

2 large egg yolks

1 egg white, for sealing

Homemade vanilla sugar (see page 136), for dusting

Start by making the filling. Dry-fry the apples: heat a frying pan on medium to low heat and "fry" the apples (without any oil or butter) until most of the moisture has evaporated. Set aside to cool.

Preheat the oven to 400°F/200°C. Line a 10- x 15-inch baking sheet with parchment paper.

To make the dough, sieve the flour onto a clean work surface, then thinly slice the cold butter into the flour. Pinch the mixture between your fingertips until it resembles coarse crumbs. Add the sugar, almonds, chocolate, and egg yolks. Work the dough with your fingers, then form into a ball. Roll out to the size of the baking sheet and carefully transfer onto the baking sheet.

Spread the filling along the bottom half of the dough, leaving an inch at the sides. Fold over the short ends by an inch. Lift one long end up and over the filling, brush with egg white and then fold over the other long end so that it overlaps in the center. Press down gently along the seams, making sure it is all sealed so none of the mixture can escape.

Bake in the oven for 1 hour, then transfer onto a wire rack to cool. Dust with vanilla sugar and serve warm.

Brauner Kirschkuchen
CHOCOLATE CHERRY CAKE

SERVES 8

2 oz ladyfingers

4 oz blanched ground almonds

2 oz dark chocolate

8½ tbsp/4 oz unsalted butter, at room temperature

¾ cup/¾ oz confectioner's sugar

4 large egg yolks, at room temperature

2 large eggs, at room temperature

4 large egg whites, at room temperature

10½ oz whole black Morello cherries, washed and dried (fresh or canned)

Place the ladyfingers in a food processor and whiz into fine crumbs. Alternatively, you can place them in a plastic food bag and smash them with a rolling pin. Transfer into a bowl and mix in the ground almonds.

Preheat the oven to 350°F/180°C. Grease a 9-inch round cake pan and line the bottom with parchment paper.

Break the chocolate into small pieces and place in a heatproof bowl. Melt the chocolate, either by heating in a microwave for 20–30 seconds or by placing the bowl over a pan of just simmering water. Make sure the bowl is not touching the water and monitor carefully. Alternatively you can melt the chocolate the way Hertha would have done (see note on page 122). Stir the chocolate until smooth and set aside to cool.

In the bowl of an electric mixer, cream the butter until light and fluffy. Gradually whisk in the confectioner's sugar a little at a time. Add the egg yolks, one at a time, whisking between each addition, then add the whole eggs, again one at a time and whisking between each addition. Stir in the cooled melted chocolate and transfer the batter into a very large bowl. Thoroughly wash the beaters. In a separate bowl, whisk the egg whites to fairly stiff peaks.

Using a large balloon whisk, fold a third of the egg whites into the batter, then fold in a third of the biscuit/almond mixture. Repeat twice more, folding in one-third of the ingredients each time.

Pour the mixture into the prepared cake pan and distribute the cherries evenly on top. Bake for 60–70 minutes, until the cake pulls away from the sides of the pan. Remove from the oven and cool in the pan before transferring to a wire rack. Serve with a generous dollop of whipped cream (see page 179).

Feine Schokoladenschnitten
DELICATE CHOCOLATE SLICES

MAKES 18

¾ oz ladyfingers

⅓ cup/2 oz rice flour

5 oz dark chocolate

10½ tbsp/5½ oz unsalted butter, at room temperature

1¼ cups/5 oz confectioner's sugar

5 large eggs, at room temperature, separated

1 cup whipping cream, whipped fairly stiffly and lightly sweetened

Preheat the oven to 320°F/160°C. Grease a 2-inch deep, 9- x 13-inch pan and line with parchment paper.

Place the ladyfingers in a food processor and whiz into fine crumbs. Alternatively, you can place them in a plastic food bag and smash them with a rolling pin. Transfer into a bowl and mix in the flour.

Break the chocolate into small pieces and place in a heatproof bowl. Melt the chocolate, either by heating in a microwave for 20–30 seconds or by placing the bowl over a pan of just simmering water. Make sure the bowl is not touching the water and monitor carefully. Alternatively you can melt the chocolate the way Hertha would have done (see note on page 122). Stir the chocolate until smooth and set aside to cool.

In the bowl of an electric mixer, cream the butter until light and fluffy. Add the confectioner's sugar, whisking all the time, then the egg yolks, one at a time, whisking between each addition. Stir in the cooled melted chocolate and transfer the batter into a very large bowl. Thoroughly wash the beaters. In a separate bowl, whisk the egg whites to stiff peaks.

Using a large balloon whisk, fold one-third of the egg whites into the batter, then fold in one-third of the flour mixture. Repeat twice more, folding in one-third of the ingredients each time.

Pour the mixture into the prepared pan. Bake for 20–25 minutes, until the cake pulls away from the sides of the pan. Remove from the oven and turn the cake out onto a wire rack to cool. Cut in half, horizontally, and spread the sweetened whipped cream over the bottom half and cover with the top half.

Mohnkuchen
POPPYSEED TART

SERVES 6

FOR THE DOUGH

1¼ cups/5 oz all-purpose flour

5½ tbsp/2½ oz unsalted butter, cold, and extra for greasing

¼ cup/2 oz superfine sugar

Pinch ground cinnamon

Grated zest of ½ lemon

1 large egg yolk, beaten

FOR THE FILLING

3 large eggs, separated

1 cup/4 oz confectioner's sugar

4 oz ground poppyseeds

¾ oz raisins

1 oz candied lemon peel, very finely chopped

Grated zest of 1 medium lemon

Confectioner's sugar, for dusting

Lightly grease an 8-inch springform pan.

Sieve the flour on to a clean work surface then thinly slice the cold butter into the flour. Pinch the mixture between your fingertips until it resembles coarse crumbs. Add the sugar, cinnamon, the lemon zest and beaten egg yolk, and swiftly knead everything into a dough, shape into a disc, wrap in plastic wrap and place into the refrigerator to chill for at least 30 minutes and up to 1 hour.

Preheat the oven to 375°F/190°C. Remove the pastry from the fridge and let it stand for 5 minutes. Using your knuckles, press the dough into the pan so that it is evenly distributed over the base. If the dough is still too hard, wait just a few more minutes. Bake in the center of the oven for 10 minutes.

Meanwhile prepare the filling. Whisk the egg yolks with ¾ cup of the confectioner's sugar until very light and fluffy and transfer to a large bowl. Add the poppyseeds, raisins, candied lemon peel, and the zest. Thoroughly wash the beaters.

In a separate bowl, whip the egg whites to soft peaks, add the remaining confectioner's sugar and whisk to firm, but not stiff, peaks. Gently fold the egg whites into the poppyseed mixture using a spatula.

Remove the partially baked base from the oven and reduce the temperature to 350°F/180°C. Pour the filling over the base and return to the oven. Bake for about 45 minutes, until the top turns golden and the cake pulls away from the sides of the pan. Transfer to a cooling rack. Leave in the pan for 5 minutes, before removing the springform ring. Cool completely and dust with confectioner's sugar.

Sacherschnitten
SACHER SLICES

MAKES 10 SLICES

FOR THE BATTER

2½–3 oz dark chocolate

6 tbsp/3 oz unsalted butter, at room temperature

Scant ¾ cup/3 oz confectioner's sugar

3 large eggs, at room temperature, separated

3½ oz apricot jam, warmed

⅓ cup/1½ oz all-purpose flour

FOR THE GLAZE

3½ oz (50% cocoa) chocolate

3½ tbsp/1¾ oz unsalted butter, at room temperature

Start by making the batter. Break the chocolate into small pieces and place in a heatproof bowl. Melt the chocolate, either by heating in a microwave for 20–30 seconds or by placing the bowl over a pan of just simmering water. Make sure the bowl is not touching the water and monitor carefully. Alternatively you can melt the chocolate the way Hertha would have done (see note on page 122). Stir the chocolate until smooth and set aside to cool. Preheat the oven to 350°F/180°C.

In the bowl of an electric mixer, cream the butter until light and fluffy, then whisk in the confectioner's sugar gradually until the mixture is light and fluffy. Stir in the cooled melted chocolate and then the egg yolks, one at a time. Thoroughly wash the beaters. In a separate bowl, whisk the egg whites to fairly stiff peaks.

Using a large balloon whisk, fold one-third of the egg whites into the batter, then fold in one-third of the flour. Repeat twice more, folding in one-third of the ingredients each time.

Grease and flour a 1-lb loaf pan. Pour the mixture into the prepared pan and bake for 50–55 minutes, until the cake pulls away from the sides of the pan. At the end of cooking time, turn off the oven, open the door, and leave the cake to cool in the oven for about 10 minutes. Then tip the cake out on a wire rack to cool completely.

Spread the warm jam over the top of the cake and while it is setting, make the glaze. Break the chocolate into small pieces and melt in a bowl over a pan of hot but not boiling water. Make sure the base of the bowl does not touch the water. Stir and when melted, remove from the heat. Stir in the butter. Pour the glaze evenly over the cake and set aside to firm up.

To cut the cake, heat the blade of a serrated knife under hot running water, and dry it well (this is to avoid cracking the glaze). Cut into thin slices.

Schlagrahm
PERFECT WHIPPED CREAM

MAKES 2 CUPS

1 cup whipping cream

1–1½ tbsp superfine sugar

Splash of light rum or
Grand Marnier (optional)

Chill a mixing bowl and electric mixer beaters in the fridge
for at least an hour.

Pour the cream into the chilled bowl and whisk, gradually
adding the sugar while whisking all the time, until the
cream starts to thicken into soft peaks. Test for sweetness and
adjust accordingly.

> **NOTE**
>
> If the cream is being used as a filling, you can add rum or Grand
> Marnier for additional flavor. Whipped cream is popular in
> Viennese cuisine and used often, not least of all with a *Schwarzen
> Kaffee*, an espresso coffee served after lunch.

Torten

TORTES

In an Austrian household, tortes are usually made for special occasions only: birthdays, engagements, anniversaries. In Tante Hertha's days, you would also serve a torte after a formal lunch. Another equally elegant invite would be a request to *komm zum Schwarzen*, the literal translation of which is "to come for a black coffee," signifying the time after lunch, usually at 2 pm, where coffee, often accompanied by freshly whipped cream, and a beautifully presented torte, would be served. Lunch would have taken place in the dining room, but for coffee, society ladies would meet for light conversation in the sun-filled salon, as Hertha's generation would have called a formal drawing room.

The salons of Hertha and her contemporaries were filled with family portraits covering faded pale pink or yellow painted walls, Biedermeier furniture, perhaps a card table in the corner, and a formality long faded away, gone with the endless summers and a time when immediate and extended family were as close as best friends, eager to catch up on the latest news. As a young girl visiting aunts and cousins, I remember the austere but comforting salons, impeccable and never-changing, somehow peaceful and familiar in their constancy.

Altwiener Topfentorte
OLD-WORLD VIENNA CURD TORTE

MAKES 8–10 SLICES

Extra-fine breadcrumbs, for dusting the cake pan

8½ tbsp/4 oz unsalted butter, plus extra for greasing

1 cup/4 oz confectioner's sugar

4 large eggs, at room temperature, separated

4 oz (20% fat) curd cheese, sieved

Grated zest of ½ lemon

Pinch of salt

1–½ tsp vanilla sugar (see page 136), plus extra for dusting

4 oz blanched ground almonds

Preheat the oven to 350°F/180°C. Grease a 9-inch round springform cake pan and lightly dust with the breadcrumbs.

In the bowl of an electric mixer, cream the butter until light and fluffy, and gradually add the confectioner's sugar until well-blended. Add one egg yolk at a time, whisking in between each addition. Now stir in the sieved curd cheese, lemon zest, salt and vanilla sugar. Set aside. Thoroughly wash the beaters.

In a separate bowl, whisk the egg whites to stiff peaks. Then alternate folding the egg whites and the ground almonds into the curd cheese/butter mixture. Do this gently and quickly.

Pour the mixture into the prepared cake pan and bake for 50–60 minutes — the cake will start to pull away from the sides of the pan when ready.

Remove from the oven and turn out onto a wire rack to cool. Once cooled, dust with vanilla-flavored confectioner's sugar and serve.

NOTE

There is nothing quite like Austrian *Topfen*, whose closest counterpart is light curd cheese, farmer's cheese, or quark. Made from milk with no extra additives or salt, *Topfen* adds a light, smooth flavor to tortes and cakes. If you are finding it hard to source in your local supermarket, most gourmet stores should have a suitable match.

Falsche Sachertorte

FAUX SACHERTORTE

MAKES 8–10 SLICES

FOR THE BATTER

10½ tbsp/5 oz unsalted butter

1¼ cups/5 oz confectioner's sugar

3 large egg yolks

5 oz dark (70% cocoa) chocolate

3½ oz ground walnuts

½ cup/2 oz all-purpose flour

5 large egg whites

FOR THE GANACHE

½ cup whipping cream

3½ tbsp/2 oz unsalted butter

4½ oz dark (70% cocoa) chocolate, coarsely chopped

Preheat the oven to 325°F/160°C . Grease and lightly flour a 9-inch round springform cake pan.

Start by making the batter. Break the chocolate into small pieces and place in a heatproof bowl. Melt the chocolate, either by heating in a microwave for 20–30 seconds or by placing the bowl over a pan of just simmering water. Make sure the bowl is not touching the water and monitor carefully. Alternatively you can melt the chocolate the way Hertha would have done (see note on page 122). Stir the chocolate until smooth and set aside to cool.

In the bowl of an electric mixer, cream the butter until light and fluffy, and gradually add two-thirds of the confectioner's sugar and beat until well blended. Add one egg yolk at a time, whisking between each addition. Then stir in the chocolate.

In a separate bowl, beat the egg whites to soft peaks using an electric mixer. Beat in the remaining one-third of confectioner's sugar until the texture is light and glossy.

Sieve the flour into a bowl with the ground walnuts. Fold half into the butter/sugar mixture, then fold in half the egg whites. Repeat with the other halves.

Pour the mixture into the prepared cake pan and bake for 55–60 minutes. Then turn off the oven but leave the cake inside with the oven door open for another 10 minutes before removing. Turn the cake out onto a wire rack when partially cooled.

While the cake is baking, make the ganache. Place the cream, butter, and chocolate in a small stainless steel saucepan and heat over medium to low heat, stirring continuously until the chocolate has melted. Remove from the heat and pour into the bowl of an electric mixer. Refrigerate for about 15 minutes. When the edges of the ganache begin to harden, take it out of the refrigerator and whisk with an electric mixer until light and fluffy.

When the cake has completely cooled, spread the ganache evenly over the top and sides. Refrigerate for at least 1 hour before serving.

Haselnußcrèmetorte

HAZELNUT CREAM TORTE

MAKES 6 SLICES

FOR THE BATTER

1½ oz fine breadcrumbs

¼ cup/1 oz all-purpose flour

5 large eggs, at room temperature, separated

1¼ cups/5½ oz confectioner's sugar

4 oz toasted ground hazelnuts

FOR THE NUT CREAM FILLING

2½ oz shelled almonds

⅓ cup/2½ oz granulated sugar

7 tbsp/3½ oz unsalted butter, at room temperature

¾ cup/3½ oz confectioner's sugar

1 large egg, beaten

1 tbsp dark rum

Preheat the oven to 375°F/190°C for 20 minutes. Grease and lightly flour an 8-inch round springform cake pan.

Start by making the batter. In a bowl, mix the breadcrumbs with the flour and set aside. In a separate bowl, whisk the egg yolks with 1 cup plus 2 tablespoons of the confectioner's sugar until light and fluffy. Wash the beaters thoroughly.

In a third bowl, beat the egg whites to soft peaks, beating in the remaining confectioner's sugar. Alternately fold the egg whites, ground hazelnuts, and flour/breadcrumbs into the sugar/egg yolk mixture.

Pour the mixture into the prepared cake pan and bake for 45–50 minutes. Remove from the oven and allow to cool in the pan. Once cooled, remove the cake from the pan.

To make the nut cream filling, start by toasting the almonds. Spread them on a baking sheet and toast for 10 minutes, or until fragrant. Remove from the oven and reduce the temperature to 300°F/150°C.

When cooled, coarsely chop the toasted nuts. Melt the sugar in a heavy saucepan over medium-low heat, stirring all the while until it caramelizes.

Remove the pan from the heat immediately and stir in the nuts. Promptly spread onto a lightly oiled baking sheet to cool. Once cooled, break into chunks, then pound coarsely (or more finely, depending on your preference) in a mortar. Reserve 4 tablespoons for the topping.

In the bowl of an electric mixer, beat the butter, confectioner's sugar and egg until light and fluffy, then stir in the caramelized almonds and the rum.

Slice the cake in half horizontally and spread two-thirds of the filling between the two layers. Spread the remaining filling over the top and sides of the cake. Sprinkle the top with the reserved caramelized almonds.

Linzertorte
LINZER TORTE

MAKES 6–8 SLICES

Scant ⅔ cup/5 oz superfine sugar

Heaped cup/5 oz all-purpose flour

5 oz ground roasted hazelnuts

1 tsp ground cinnamon

10 tbsp/5 oz cold unsalted butter, diced

Grated zest of 1 lemon

Juice of 1 lemon

3 large egg yolks

6½ oz red currant, raspberry or plum jam (red currant is the classic choice)

Preheat the oven to 350°F/180°C. Grind the roasted hazelnuts with half the sugar in a food processor until powdery – be careful not to over process as you do not want the mixture to turn into a paste.

Add the rest of the dry ingredients to the food processor, along with the diced butter. Process until the mixture resembles coarse breadcrumbs. Add the lemon zest, followed by the lemon juice and egg yolks and process again to form a dough. Form the dough into a ball, wrap in plastic wrap and refrigerate for 1 hour.

Remove the dough from the fridge and knead quickly. Take two-thirds of the dough and press it into a 9-inch round springform pan, using your knuckles to firm it down. Pull the dough 1 inch up the sides of the pan. Evenly spread the base (but not the sides) with the jam. Roll out the remaining dough to a thickness of ⅛ inch and cut it into enough ¾-inch wide strips to cover the cake. Place the strips across the top of the jam, like a lattice, trimming the strips to fit. Gently press the strips down with your fingers.

Bake for 45–50 minutes. Remove the cake from oven but do not remove it from the pan until it has cooled completely or it will crumble.

> NOTE
>
> If you like, you can brush the lattice strips with one egg yolk mixed with 1 tbsp milk. This will give the torte a shiny gloss and golden color. Make sure the glaze does not spill onto the jam!

Mohntorte Tante Fränzchen
AUNT FRÄNZCHEN'S POPPYSEED TORTE

MAKES 6–8 SLICES

14 tbsp/7 oz unsalted butter, at room temperature

1½ cups/7oz confectioner's sugar

6 large eggs, separated, at room temperature

5 oz ground poppyseeds

2 oz ground almonds

2 tbsp dark rum

2 tbsp all-purpose flour, sieved

Pinch of salt

About 5 tbsp red currant jam, warmed and cooled

1 tbsp poppyseeds, to decorate

FOR THE GLAZE

2 tbsp lemon juice

2 tbsp rum

2 cups/9 oz confectioner's sugar

1–2 tbsp boiling water

Preheat the oven to 325°F/160°C. Grease and lightly flour a 9-inch round springform cake pan. Line the bottom with parchment paper.

In the bowl of an electric mixer, cream the butter until light and fluffy. Gradually add the confectioner's sugar, whisking constantly. Add one yolk at a time, beating well between each addition, until fully incorporated. Transfer the mixture to a large bowl and mix in the ground poppyseeds, ground almonds, and rum.

In a separate bowl, whisk the egg whites to fairly stiff peaks. Using a balloon whisk, alternately fold the egg whites into the butter/sugar mixture, with the sifted flour and salt.

Pour the batter into the prepared cake pan and bake for 55–60 minutes. The cake is ready when it starts to pull away from the sides of the cake pan. Remove from the oven and turn the cake onto a wire rack to cool. You can even leave it overnight and glaze the next day so that the cake sets and mellows.

To make the glaze, mix the lemon juice and rum into the confectioner's sugar, and add just enough boiling water to form a spreadable glaze.

Slice the cake in half horizontally and spread half the jam between the two layers. Spread the remaining jam thinly over the top and sides of the cake. Once the jam has dried, spread the top and sides of the cake with your choice of glaze (either the one made here or the chocolate or lemon glazes on page 194). Sprinkle with a handful of poppyseeds to decorate.

NOTE

If you can't purchase ground poppyseeds, you can pulse them in an electric coffee grinder.

Nusstorte mit Mochacrème
NUT TORTE WITH MOCHA CREAM FILLING

MAKES 6–8 SLICES

FOR THE BATTER

1½ oz fine breadcrumbs

¼ cup/1 oz all-purpose flour

5 large eggs, at room temperature, separated

1¼ cup/5½ oz confectioner's sugar

4 oz ground walnuts

FOR THE COFFEE FILLING

10½ tbsp/5 oz unsalted butter, at room temperature

1 cup/4 oz confectioner's sugar

1 large egg yolk

¼ cup cold strong black coffee or espresso

1 tbsp vanilla sugar (optional) (see page 136)

EGG WHITE GLAZE

2–2⅓ cups/9-10½ oz confectioner's sugar

2 tsp egg white

CHOCOLATE GLAZE

Scant 3½ tbsp/2 oz unsalted butter

3½ oz (50% cocoa) chocolate

Preheat the oven to 375°F/190°C for 20 minutes. Grease and dust a 9-inch round springform cake pan with breadcrumbs (or ground almonds if you prefer).

Start by making the batter. In a bowl, mix the breadcrumbs with the flour and set aside. In a separate bowl, whisk the egg yolks with 1 cup plus 2 tablespoons of the confectioner's sugar until light and fluffy. Wash the beaters thoroughly.

In a third bowl, beat the egg whites to soft peaks, beating in the remaining confectioner's sugar. Alternately fold the egg whites, ground walnuts, and flour/breadcrumbs into the sugar/egg yolk mixture.

Pour the mixture into the prepared cake pan and bake for 45–50 minutes. Remove from the oven and allow to cool in the pan, then turn out onto a wire rack. Glaze with either the chocolate glaze or the egg white glaze.

To make the filling, cream the butter until light. Add the confectioner's sugar and continue beating until very light and fluffy, then beat in the egg yolk. Stir in the cold coffee along with the vanilla sugar.

Mix the egg white into the confectioner's sugar so that you have a spreadable icing.

Break the chocolate into small pieces and place in a heatproof bowl. Melt the chocolate, either by heating in a microwave for 20–30 seconds or by placing the bowl over a pan of just simmering water. Make sure the bowl is not touching the water and monitor carefully. Alternatively you can melt the chocolate the way Hertha would have (see note on page 122). When melted add the butter and stir to blend.

Sacher-Gugelhupf

HOTEL SACHER GUGELHOPF

MAKES 8 SLICES

FOR THE BATTER

8½ tbsp/4 oz unsalted butter, at room temperature

1⅓ cup/6 oz confectioner's sugar

4 large egg yolks, at room temperature

Grated zest of 1 lemon

3 tbsp milk

1⅔ cup/7 oz all-purpose flour

2 tsp baking powder

4 large egg whites, at room temperature

2 oz raisins, dusted with flour

Preheat the oven to 350°F/180°C for 30 minutes. Generously grease and lightly flour a 8-inch ring mold.

In the bowl of an electric mixer, cream the butter until light and fluffy, and gradually add the confectioner's sugar until well-blended. Add one egg yolk at a time, whisking in between each addition. Now stir in the lemon zest, milk and ¼ cup of the flour.

In a separate bowl, sieve the remaining flour with the baking powder. In another bowl, beat the egg whites to stiff peaks.

Using a spatula, fold one third of the flour mixture into the whipped butter, egg and sugar mixture, followed by the egg whites. Repeat twice more. Finally and swiftly, fold in the dusted raisins.

Pour the mixture into the prepared cake pan and bake for about 1 hour, until deep golden in color. Then remove the cake from the oven and allow to cool in the pan for 10–15 minutes before turning onto a wire rack to cool. When the cake has cooled completely, ice it with chocolate glaze (see page 194).

Orangenbuttercrèmetorte
ORANGE BUTTERCREAM TORTE

MAKES 6–8 SLICES

FOR THE BATTER

6 large egg yolks, at room temperature

1 cup/5 oz confectioner's sugar

4 large egg whites, at room temperature

5 oz ground almonds

¾ oz fine breadcrumbs, soaked in the juice of 1 orange

FOR THE FILLING

1 tsp all-purpose flour

4 tbsp fresh orange juice

2 tbsp rum

4 large egg yolks

7 tbsp/3½ oz unsalted butter, at room temperature

¾ cup/3½ oz confectioner's sugar

Preheat the oven to 375°F/190°C. Grease and lightly flour a 9-inch round springform cake pan.

In the bowl of an electric mixer, lightly beat the egg yolks. Add the confectioner's sugar and beat to a very light color. Thoroughly wash the beaters.

In a separate bowl, beat the egg whites to stiff peaks and gently fold them into the egg yolk/sugar mixture, adding the ground almonds and moistened breadcrumbs alternately.

Pour the mixture into the prepared cake pan and bake for 40–45 minutes. Remove from the oven and allow the cake to cool in the pan for 15 minutes before turning it over onto a wire rack to cool.

To make the filling, mix the flour with the orange juice and rum in a small saucepan off the heat. Turn the heat on low, and add the egg yolks, stirring constantly until thickened. Remove from the heat and set aside to cool.

Meanwhile, in the bowl of an electric mixer, cream the butter until light and fluffy, and gradually beat in the confectioner's sugar. Very gradually beat in the cooled egg mixture, until fully incorporated.

Slice the cake in half horizontally and spread the filling between the two layers. Cover with one of the glazes on page 194.

Schokotorte

CHOCOLATE TORTE

MAKES 6–8 SLICES

2½ oz dark (70% cocoa) chocolate

2½ oz ground almonds

2 tbsp fine breadcrumbs

Pinch of salt

5½ tbsp/2½ oz unsalted butter, at room temperature

⅔ cup/2½ oz confectioner's sugar

4 large eggs, at room temperature, separated

Whipped cream, to serve

For the ganache, see page 185

Preheat the oven to 350°F/180°C. Grease and lightly flour a 9-inch round springform cake pan.

Break the chocolate into small pieces and place in a heatproof bowl. Melt the chocolate, either by heating in a microwave for 20–30 seconds or by placing the bowl over a pan of just simmering water. Make sure the bowl is not touching the water and monitor carefully. Alternatively you can melt the chocolate the way Hertha would have done (see note on page 122). Stir the chocolate until smooth and set aside to cool.

In a bowl, mix the ground almonds, breadcrumbs and salt and set aside. In a separate bowl, cream the butter until light. Add the confectioner's sugar, one tablespoon at a time, beating between each addition, until the mixture is light and fluffy. Then stir in the cooled chocolate.

In a separate bowl, whisk the egg whites to stiff peaks and gently fold into the creamed butter mixture one-third at a time, alternating with the ground almond mixture, until all has been incorporated.

Pour the mixture into the prepared cake pan and bake for about 50 minutes. To test the cake, insert a toothpick into its center. If it comes out clean and the cake pulls away from the sides of the pan, it is ready. Turn off the heat but leave the cake in the oven with the door open for 10 minutes. Remove the cake from the oven and when it has cooled more, turn it out onto a wire rack to cool.

Slice the cake in half horizontally and spread half the ganache between the two cake layers. Spread the remaining ganache over the top and sides of the cake. For a fancy effect, sprinkle chopped pistachios on top. Cut into generous slices and serve with whipped cream.

Topfentorte Lene

LENE'S CHEESE CURD TORTE

MAKES 8 SLICES

2 cups/9 oz all-purpose flour

1 tsp baking powder

1 large egg yolk

3–4 tbsp sour cream

1 cup/4 oz confectioner's sugar

4 tbsp/2 oz unsalted butter, cold

FOR THE FILLING

1 tbsp all-purpose flour

2 tbsp cornstarch

1 tsp baking powder

Generous ¾ cup sour cream

2 large egg yolks

Juice and zest of ½ lemon

13½ oz curd cheese (20% fat)

4 tbsp granulated sugar

2½ oz raisins

3 large egg whites

Grease and lightly flour a 9-inch round springform cake pan.

Sift the flour with the baking powder on a clean work surface. Thinly slice the cold butter into the flour and pinch the mixture between your fingertips until it resembles coarse crumbs.

Mix in the sugar, then make a well in the center. In a bowl, mix the egg yolk with the sour cream and pour into the center. Knead into a dough using the heels of your hands for 2–3 minutes. The dough should be smooth and not stick to the work surface. Shape the dough into a ball, wrap it in plastic wrap and refrigerate for 1 hour.

Remove the dough from the fridge and roll it out to a circle that is 2 inches larger than the base of the cake pan. Transfer to the pan and gently press it onto the base and sides. Chill for 15 minutes while preparing the filling. Preheat the oven to 350°F/180°C.

To make the filling, mix the flour with the cornstarch and baking powder and set aside. Press the curd cheese through a sieve into a large bowl. Add the sugar, lemon juice and zest, sour cream, egg yolks, mixing it all together with a wooden spoon. Then sift the flour mixture over the mixture in the bowl. Finally, add the raisins and fold them in.

Beat the egg whites until soft peaks form. Using a spatula, gently fold the egg whites into the cheese mixture. Empty the filling into the prepared pan and bake for 10 minutes, then reduce the heat to 325°F/160°C and bake for another 45 minutes, until golden and the cake begins to pull away from the sides of the pan. Turn off the heat, open the oven door, and leave the cake inside for 10 minutes.

Place the cake on a cooling rack and cool for 10 minutes, before removing the sides of the pan.

Tante Herthas Geburtstagstorte
TANTE HERTHA'S BIRTHDAY TORTE

SERVES 6

FOR THE BATTER

7 oz dark (70% cocoa) chocolate

14 tbsp/7 oz unsalted butter, at room temperature (not soft)

1½ cups/7 oz confectioner's sugar

4 large eggs, separated

½ cup/2 oz all-purpose flour

FOR THE PRALINE

Scant ½ cup/3½ oz granulated sugar

3½ oz hazelnuts, toasted

TOASTING HAZELNUTS

Preheat the oven to 350°F/180°C. Spread the nuts on a baking sheet and toast for 10 minutes, or until fragrant. Remove from the oven.

Preheat the oven to 325°F/160°C. Grease and lightly flour a 8-inch round springform cake pan.

Break the chocolate into small pieces and place in a heatproof bowl. Melt the chocolate, either by heating in a microwave for 20–30 seconds or by placing the bowl over a pan of just simmering water. Make sure the bowl is not touching the water and monitor carefully. Alternatively you can melt the chocolate the way Hertha would have (see note on page 122). Stir the chocolate until smooth and set aside to cool.

In the bowl of an electric mixer, cream the butter until light and fluffy, and gradually add the confectioner's sugar, increasing the speed for 1–2 minutes. Add one egg yolk at a time, whisking in between each addition. Now stir in the melted chocolate until well blended.

In a separate bowl, beat the egg whites to stiff peaks. Using a large ballon whisk, fold the egg whites into the butter/chocolate mixture.

Divide the mixture into two portions, with one portion slightly larger than the other. Set aside the larger portion in a cool place (but not in the refrigerator as it needs to be spreadable). Stir the flour into the smaller portion and pour this into the prepared cake pan.

Bake for 30–33 minutes, then remove from oven and cool in the pan on a rack for 10 minutes. Then remove from the pan and cool on the rack completely before spreading the remaining mixture on the top and sides.

To make the praline (this can be made in advance), coarsely chop the toasted hazelnuts. Melt the sugar in a medium saucepan, stirring all the while, until it caramelizes. Remove from the heat and stir in the hazelnuts. Immediately spread onto a lightly oiled baking sheet to cool. Once cooled, break into chunks, then pound coarsely in a mortar (or more finely, depending on personal preference, on a wooden board with a sharp knife). Sprinkle the praline on top of the cake. Refrigerate for several hours before serving.

Crèmes und Marmeladen

PUDDINGS AND JAMS

In the early 1950s some time after the war, Tante Hertha began a small catering business, her reputation as a fine cook preceding her among a large circle of friends and family. Her signature creations were her heavenly jams and marmalades. Orders were placed every year and Hertha, at this time living with a cousin and an aunt, singlehandedly began the process of seasonal jam-making. My mother can remember the waft of oranges lingering throughout the beautiful apartment during Vienna's icy cold winter months when bitter oranges from Seville became available. In mid to late summer, Hertha would purchase freshly plucked apricots, plums, strawberries, and raspberries from the Naschmarkt for her jams. An annual vacation was always scheduled for late August when the final glasses of jams had been sealed and stored under beds, on top of armoires, in corners of the kitchen, the pantry, the salon. The coveted jams and marmalades were collected upon Hertha's return; Hertha refreshed from her vacation, her clients happy, and her cousin Christl relieved by the return of a slightly more spacious apartment for another six months.

Dali-Crème

VANILLA MOUSSE WITH RASPBERRY OR STRAWBERRY COULIS

SERVES 4

FOR THE MOUSSE

Scant ¾ cup whipping cream

⅓ cup/2½ oz superfine sugar

¼ tsp vanilla extract

4 large egg yolks

⅓ oz gelatin powder

2 tbsp lemon juice

Grated zest of ½ lemon

FOR THE COULIS

9 oz fresh or frozen raspberries, defrosted

1–2 tbsp Framboise or Kirsch (optional)

⅔ cup/2½ oz confectioner's sugar, or to taste

Start by making the mousse. Whisk the whipping cream with ½ tablespoon of the sugar and vanilla extract until it starts to thicken and form soft peaks. Refrigerate until ready to use.

In the bowl of an electric mixer, combine the egg yolks and gradually beat in the remaining sugar. Set the bowl over a pan of simmering water, making sure the base of the bowl does not touch the water, and whisk with a balloon whisk for 5–8 minutes, until the mixture is thick. Remove from the heat and whisk on medium speed for 5 minutes.

Measure ½ cup cold water into a heat-resistant bowl and sprinkle the gelatin into it to soften. Then place the bowl over a pan of simmering water to melt, while stirring all the time.

Gradually pour the melted gelatin into the egg and sugar mixture and whisk on a low speed. Whisk in the lemon juice and the grated zest until incorporated.

Set the mixture over ice, stirring regularly until it begins to set, then immediately remove from the ice and gently fold in the whipped cream with a balloon whisk or spatula. Pour into a rinsed 4-cup jello mold, cover and chill for at least 6 hours. Keeps for up to two days in the fridge.

To make the coulis, purée the raspberries in a blender with the alcohol of your choice. Strain through a fine sieve, using the underside of a spoon to push through the fruit. Stir in the confectioner's sugar and pour into a small jug, ready to serve. Refrigerate before serving.

Eiercognac Tante Putzi
AUNT PUTZI'S EGG COGNAC

MAKES 6 CUPS

3 cups whole milk

Generous 2 cups/9 oz confectioner's sugar

1 oz vanilla sugar (see page 136)

5 large egg yolks

1 cup vodka

Rinse a medium-size saucepan in water (but do not dry). Pour in the milk, along with ¾ cup of the confectioner's sugar and the vanilla sugar. Slowly bring to a boil, then reduce the heat and simmer for 30 minutes, uncovered. Remove from the heat and set aside to cool. Then strain the milk through a sieve into a large jug or bowl to leave the skin behind.

In the bowl of an electric mixer, whisk the egg yolks with the remaining confectioner's sugar (1¼ cup) until pale. Ladle a quarter of the strained milk into the mixture, and whisk on the lowest setting. Now add the remaining milk and the vodka and whisk very briefly to incorporate.

Transfer to a sterilized bottle and refrigerate for four to five days before sampling this delicious tipple. Keeps well, refrigerated, for up to four months.

Marillen/fruchtkompott

APRICOT/OTHER FRUIT COMPOTE

SERVES 6

2¼ lb ripe apricots (or fruit of your choice)

1⅓ cup/10½ oz granulated sugar

Wash and pit the apricots, then cut them in half. Place them in a bowl and pour the sugar over them. Cover with a lid and let them stand at room temperature overnight.

The next day, transfer the apricots and sugar to a pan and cook over low heat to start with, then increase the heat gradually until the fruit comes to a boil. Reduce the heat and simmer for 20–25 minutes. Turn off the heat then set aside to cool.

This compote is delicious served with a dollop of crème fraîche and for an extra flavorful touch, sprinkled with chopped pistachios or coarsely-chopped roasted walnuts. Compotes also accompany many pancake-style dishes such as *Kaiserschmarren* (see page 148) or *Palatschinken* (see page 149).

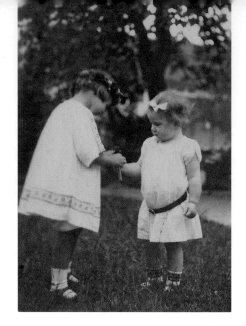

Orangenschaum
ORANGE FOAM JELLO

MAKES 2 CUPS

1½ cups/12 oz superfine sugar

¾ oz gelatin powder

Zest of 1 lemon

Juice of 3 oranges (1¼ cups)

Juice of 2 small lemons
(⅔ cup)

Pour ⅓ cup of water in a pan and tip in the sugar. Place on low heat until the sugar has dissolved, stirring occasionally. Remove from the heat.

Pour a scant ½ cup hot but not boiling water in a heat-resistant bowl and sprinkle the gelatin into it, stirring with a fork until dissolved. Add this to the hot sugar water, stirring vigorously to incorporate the gelatin into the sugar water. Stir in the lemon zest and set aside to cool.

Strain the orange and lemon juices through a sieve, then whisk the juice into the cooled gelatin mixture using an electric mixer. Whisk on high speed for several minutes until the liquid turns light and foamy. Pour into a 2-cup mold or plastic container and refrigerate for several hours or overnight.

Schokoladencrème

SOFT CHOCOLATE PUDDING

SERVES 8

Butter, for greasing

Confectioner's sugar or cocoa powder, for dusting

5 oz (50% cocoa) chocolate

1½ cups whipping cream

6 large egg yolks

6 tbsp granulated sugar

Prepare eight 2-inch deep, 3-inch round ramekins. Lightly grease and dust with confectioner's sugar or cocoa powder.

Break the chocolate into small pieces in an ovensafe bowl and place in the center of a preheated 200°F/100°C oven until it has just melted to a silky smooth texture, about 10–15 minutes. Remove from oven, stir until smooth and set aside to cool. Increase the oven temperature to 325°F/160°C.

In a stainless steel saucepan over very low heat, slowly bring the cream just to the brink of boiling. Pour in the melted chocolate, stir, and set aside to cool.

Using an electric mixer, whisk the egg yolks with the sugar, starting on a low speed and gradually increasing to medium and then high, until thick, creamy, and pale. In a slow stream, add the cream/chocolate mixture, whisking at the lowest speed.

Divide the mixture equally into the ramekins and place them in a roasting pan. Carefully pour boiling water into the pan (not into the ramekins!) until the water is ½ inch up the sides of the ramekins. Bake for 35–40 minutes, or until risen and the tops feel firm to the touch.

Topfencrème

QUARK CRÈME

SERVES 4

1 cup quark (farmer's cheese)

1 cup sour cream

1 cup plain yogurt

3 tbsp light brown sugar

2 tsp lemon juice, or to taste

In a mixing bowl, whisk the quark with an electric mixer, then whisk in the sour cream, yogurt, sugar, and lemon juice, to taste. The consistency should be that of a thick cream.

This is a delicious light crème, served either on its own or with seasonal berries. It can also be poured over vanilla ice cream. If you make a mistake and it turns out too runny, this is not a problem – refrigerate and have it as a yogurt type drink instead.

Schokoladenreis
CHOCOLATE RICE PUDDING

SERVES 6–8

1 cup/7 oz short-grain rice or Italian arborio rice

3 cups milk

5 tbsp/2½ oz unsalted butter

⅓ cup/2½ oz granulated sugar

3–4 large eggs, separated

3 oz dark (70% cocoa) chocolate, grated

Confectioner's sugar, for sprinkling (optional)

Preheat the oven to 350°F/180°C. Generously grease an 8-inch round soufflé dish.

Rinse the rice under hot running water. Pour the milk in a saucepan and cook the rice in the milk until al dente. Set aside to cool.

In the bowl of an electric mixer, cream the butter with the sugar until light and fluffy. Add the egg yolks, one at the time, whisking between each addition. Thoroughly wash the beaters, then in a separate bowl, whisk the egg whites to stiff peaks.

Stir the cooled rice into the creamed butter mixture and fold in the beaten egg whites. Place half the mixture into the prepared soufflé dish. Sprinkle over the grated chocolate and cover with the rest of the rice mixture. Sprinkle the top with sugar, if desired. Bake for 40 minutes, or until top is light golden. For complete decadence, serve with a dollop of whipped cream.

Jams

There are a few basic rules for successful jam-making:

✳ Use impeccably clean, stainless steel equipment and pots, ensuring there are no food odors.

✳ The jars in which you store the jam must be made of glass, sterilized and filled with jam while the jam is still hot.

✳ To sterilize the jars and lids, wash them in hot soapy water, then rinse thoroughly with hot water. Place clean jars lying down in a large pan, cover completely with cold water, cover pan, bring to a boil and continue boiling, covered for 20 minutes. Then with tongs and rubber gloves, remove them from the pan, tip out the water and drain. Stand upright on a clean towel to air dry.

✳ To sterilize the jars in a dishwasher, use the rinse cycle at the hottest temperature, and do not use dishwashing detergent.

✳ Use a silver spoon (without superstition!) for testing whether the jam has reached "setting point." To do this, drop a teaspoon of the mixture onto a cold saucer, which had been chilled in the freezer for a few minutes, then return it to the freezer for 5 minutes, until the jam has cooled to room temperature. If it is ready, a skin will have formed on the surface of the jam and it will wrinkle when you push it with your finger.

✳ The fruit should be as freshly picked as possible and slightly under-ripe as this is the stage when the pectin content is at its highest.

✳ Filled jars are best stored in a cool, dry, dark place for up to one year. Once opened, refrigerate and keep for up to six months.

Marillenmarmelade

APRICOT JAM

MAKES 3–4 1-CUP (8-FL OZ) JARS

2¼ lb ripe, pitted apricots

2¼ cup/17½ oz granulated sugar

Wash the apricots, halve them and remove the pits and any blemishes, then weigh them. Cut the fruit into small pieces.

Put the fruit in a stainless steel saucepan and bring gently to a boil. Simmer, uncovered, until the fruit is soft, about 15 minutes. Stir frequently.

Add the sugar to the pan, increasing the heat to high, stirring so that the sugar dissolves quickly (the sugar must dissolve before the mixture comes to a boil).

After this point, bring the jam to a quick boil, stirring regularly to prevent the jam sticking to the base of the pan, particularly toward the end of cooking time. The mixture should be thick and ready to set. This will take approximately 30–40 minutes.

Check the setting point of the jam (see page 214 for setting point). Then remove from heat and immediately transfer into hot, sterilized jars (see page 214). Wipe the rims clean and seal once the jam is cold.

Himbeermarmelade

RASPBERRY JAM

MAKES 2–3 1-CUP (8-FL OZ) JARS

2½ cup/17½ oz granulated sugar

17½ oz raspberries, fresh or frozen

1 tbsp lemon juice

OR TRY THIS...

Instead of just raspberries, use a mix of 9 oz raspberries and 9 oz red currants. In this case, both fruits will have to be harvested during their growing season. For this version, the lemon juice will be omitted but the sugar quantity stays the same.

Preheat the oven to 300°F/150°C.

Warm the sugar in the oven in a heat-resistant bowl for 8–10 minutes.

In a large, shallow stainless steel saucepan, combine the fruit and the lemon juice, and simmer gently for 5 minutes, stirring it once or twice. Tip in the warmed sugar all in one go. Stir to dissolve the sugar, then increase the heat and bring to a boil.

Boil uncovered, without stirring, for about 12 minutes, until the jam sets when tested (see page 214 for setting point). Remove from heat and immediately transfer to hot, sterilized jars (see page 214). Wipe the rims clean and seal once the jam is cold.

Orangenmarmelade

ORANGE MARMALADE

**MAKES 12 1-CUP
(8-FL OZ) JARS**

2¼ lb Seville oranges

8 cups water

10 cups/4½ lb granulated
sugar

Wash the oranges (as you will be using the peel). Cut them into quarters and shred them very finely, using a mandolin or the thinnest slicer on a food processor (do not peel the oranges). Reserve the seeds: keep them in a bowl and cover them with 1 cup of the water. Cover with plastic wrap and let stand overnight.

Put the shredded oranges in a large bowl, pour over the remaining water, cover with plastic wrap, and let stand overnight.

The following day, wrap the seeds in a piece of muslin and secure with a knot. Pour the water in which the seeds have been standing into the bowl with the shredded oranges.

Transfer the shredded oranges and their juice to a large stainless steel pan. Drop the muslin bag in the pan. Bring to a boil, then lower the heat and simmer, covered, for about 30–40 minutes, until the fruit is medium-soft, then discard the muslin bag and its contents.

While still on low heat, add the sugar, stirring until it has dissolved. Then bring to a boil again, uncovered, without stirring, for about 30 minutes, or until the marmalade reaches setting point (see page 214). Then remove the pan from the heat. Pour into hot, sterilized jars (see page 214) using a ladle. Wipe the rims clean and seal once the jam is cold.

Powidel

PLUM PRESERVE

MAKES 2 CUPS

10½ oz pitted prunes

2 tsp grated zest of an orange or lemon

2½ oz homemade (see page 216) or store-bought raspberry jam

2 tsp lemon juice

In a pan, bring the prunes with a scant $\frac{2}{3}$ cup water and the orange/lemon zest to a boil, then reduce the heat and simmer for 20 minutes.

Remove from the heat and when cooled, pulse in a food processor until smooth. Transfer to a bowl and stir in the raspberry jam with the lemon juice.

Store in a glass jar with a tight-fitting lid. Refrigerate and allow the flavors to "mellow" for a few days before sampling. Once opened, the plum preserve will keep for several weeks when refrigerated.

This is a modern method; the traditional recipe would have taken almost a week to prepare!

$\mathscr{I}ndex$

Acknowledgements

To our friends at New Holland, with a very special thank you to Steve Connolly for his effusive *jawohl!* to the concept, to the Rights ladies and to our publisher, the calm and collected Clare Sayer. Also to the wonderful team of creative collaborators: Jacqui Caulton, a true artist and brilliant designer; Tara Fisher; Roisin Nield; Annie Rigg; and our copy editor, my lovely and highly exacting friend Corinne Masciocchi.

To:

Alexandra Koken, the Audrey Hepburn look-alike who first translated the worn pages of Tante Hertha's collection into English; the artists Barbara and Zafer Baran for so delicately handling these nearly century-old pages into legible working copies, and to Peter Mikl and Waltraud Strummer of the Austrian Cultural Forum for graciously hosting us to celebrate the cookbook's debut. To Michel Moushabeck of Interlink Publishing, close colleague and friend and now, with much joy, our US publisher.

Sarah al-Hamad, a dear friend and inspiration for the book. Without Sarah and her own historical cookbook, we would not have had the self-belief to go forward. To her partner Matthew Bishop, another *Feinschmecker* who approved of the testing with gusto. Photographer and friend Jon Meade on his hotshot assignment to Vienna, managing to encapsulate the essence of the city in just one day with over 200 incredible shots (and a few Demel chocolate boxes to spare). And to our very special muse, Michelle Lo.

The many Londoners, New Yorkers, and Torontonians full of enthusiasm and encouragement (and eagerly, patiently awaiting further recipe sampling). Among them: David Cormack; Jeannine and Harrison Dillon; Gary Holmes; Lisa Honig for our imaginative cover and title pitches; Marla Hurov; Petra Kwan; Kristin Lauhn-Jensen; Sandy Levine; Joanne Shurvell; Eva Svec; Mindy Tenenbaum; Sandra Worden and Lori Zajkowski; and with eternal gratitude to Lisa Hostein, who for over twenty-five years, from London, Ontario to London, England, has so tirelessly reiterated: "Just get in there and write!"

Anne Bieker; Helga Hödl; Tatjana Panceva; Anna and Sharon Schauenstein, Vlasta Svec, and the dashing Chris Oldfield for their priceless recipe homages. To the original girls from Graz: Kerstin Bieker, Franscesca Bubna-Kasteliz, Judith Scholes.

Most importantly, to our family, distanced only by the geography of fate. To the Austrians and *Ausgewanderten*, most notably Georg von Baich for his first intrepid photo shoot to a somewhat rainy Vienna and Graz, handled like a pro; Paul and Marie von Baich, and Theodor and Ina Baich for their enchanting heartfelt recollections of Tante Hertha; and to the beloved Tante Li Bubna. To cousins Barbara and her husband Philip Manby; and Andrew Lowe, the most unique and generous man gracing our English/Scottish family tree. To Bernard and Bryan, always.